To

Lois

with warm

regards

June Kelly

Ma Chance's
French Caribbean Creole Cooking

JEANNE LOUISE DUZANT CHANCE

Ma Chance's French Caribbean Creole Cooking

Art by Romare Bearden
Edited and compiled by June Kelly

G. P. PUTNAM'S SONS   NEW YORK

G. P. Putnam's Sons
Publishers Since 1838
200 Madison Avenue
New York, NY 10016

Library of Congress Cataloging in Publication Data

Chance, Jeanne Louise Duzant.
Ma Chance's French Caribbean creole cooking.

Includes index.
1. Cookery, Caribbean.   2. Cookery, Creole.
I. Kelly, June.   II. Title.   III. Title: French Caribbean
creole cooking.
TX716.C37C47   1985   641.597297′6   85-3376
ISBN 0-399-13035-7

Printed in the United States of America
1   2   3   4   5   6   7   8   9   10

ACKNOWLEDGMENTS

Lorna St. Hill, who tested these recipes and made
useful comments and suggestions.
Michael Chisolm, an invaluable food consultant.
Elinor Bowles, who helped me reflect on my
life in St. Martin.
Romare Bearden, who encouraged me so that
my dream could come true.

A special thanks to June Kelly, who prepared this book
for publication with diligence and dedication.

I also want to thank Lana Johnson, Lee Glenn, Barbara
Kulicke, Charles Storer, Adrienne Ingrum, our editor
at The Putnam Publishing Group, and the New York
Botanical Garden.

To my beloved family: my mother, Eliza, my husband, Leon, and to Philomine, Suzanne, Charles, Bernard, Patricia, Mark, Alyssa, Shauntée, and Elliot, and to my dear friends Claire and Clemencia.

Contents

St. Martin

Anse des Pères

Pte Arago

Baie de
la Potence

80

Pte du Bluff

Baie aux
Cailles

Petite Baie

Pte Plum
13

Falaise des Oiseaux

Pte des
Pierres à Chaux

Baie Rouge

Anse des
Sables

MARIGOT

Baie Nettlé

Baie de Marigot

Peninsule des
Terres Basses

80

Anse aux
Acajoux

S'Jam

Pointe du
Canonnier

PORT DE PLAISANCE

PK 273

D 208

Baie Longue

GRAND ETANG DE SIMSONBAAI

4,6

Grand
Ilet

26

Mullet Pond Bay

Aérodrome
Princess Juliana

Simsonbaai

Simson Baai

5,4

121

Kool Baai

LEGEND

National road	———
Departmental road	═══
Distance in kilometers	5,4
Altitude	· 124
Airport	✈

Copyright by **PEP**

Made possible with the cooperation of La
Préfecture de la Guadeloupe and La
Direction Départementale de L'Equipement.

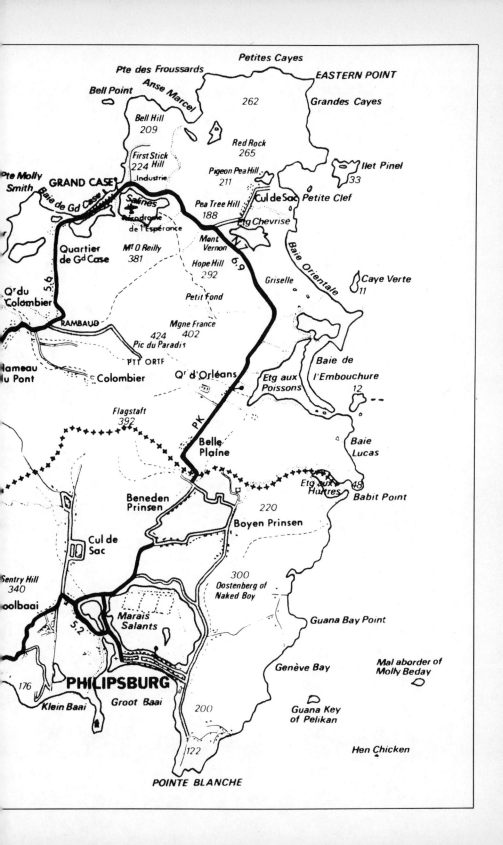

About St. Martin

St. Martin is a tropical island embraced by the Caribbean Sea and the Atlantic Ocean. It is a mecca for sun-lovers and vacationers from around the world, especially the United States, Canada, and western Europe.

The island is 37 square miles divided roughly in half between the French side and the Dutch side. Each side of the island is considered part of its mother country. Thus, Saint Martin is France, and Sint Maarten is the Netherlands.

The first-known inhabitants of St. Martin were the Arawak and Carib Indians. The Carib gave the island its first recorded name, Sualouiga, which meant salt lands. The harvesting of salt from shallow briny ponds made an important contribution to the island's history and economy for many generations.

It is said that St. Martin was given its present name by Christopher Columbus when he sailed past the island on November 11, 1493, the feast day of St. Martin of Tours.

Spaniards are said to have established the first European settlement on St. Martin early in the seventeenth century, but they withdrew from the island ten years later. Legend has it that they were followed by two small groups of sailors, one French and the other Dutch, who agreed to share the island peaceably. This agreement was reached on March 24, 1648, at a meeting on a hilltop that still bears the name Mont des Accords.

According to legend, the island was divided as a result of a walking contest between a Frenchman and a Dutchman that same year; the Frenchman paced off a greater share of the island.

Residents of the island and visitors still move back and forth freely between the two sides of the island without having to go through customs, immigration, or other formalities. The boundary between France and the Netherlands on this beautiful island is marked simply by signs of welcome—"Bienvenue Partie Française" and "Welkom aan de Nederlandse Kant."

The French side of the island, a sub-prefecture of Guadeloupe, is 21 square miles and has a population of about 12,000 people. The terrain reminds a visitor of the French countryside, of Brittany perhaps—pastures set off by stone walls on gently sloping hillsides. The coastline offers deep bays and coves and white sand beaches that encircle the island.

The descendants of early involuntary immigrants brought from West Africa (slavery was abolished in 1848) are today the majority in St. Martin. The villages have a unique West Indian charm with a strong flavor of France. There are open markets typical of the Caribbean; bakeries and boutiques typical of Paris; open-air cafés that remind a visitor of the French Riviera; an ambience that soothes and seems to ignore the clock.

Marigot, the capital of St. Martin, is a Caribbean port city, with large and small ocean-going vessels and inter-island schooners standing at anchor in the harbor or tied up at the bayfront.

Saturday in Marigot is market day, and local people come from all parts of the island to offer goods and buy provisions for the coming week. In the many open stalls, there are bananas, plaintains, fish of many species, mutton, goat, breadfruits, christophenes, dasheen, cassavas, mangoes, papayas, soursops, sugar apples, and pigeon peas. There are beautiful tropical flowers for sale, and the vendors and shoppers, mostly women, dressed in bright colors, gossip and bargain vociferously in the patois of the island. As the shoppers leave, their purchases are neatly packed in baskets they balance on their heads. It is a colorful event that reflects and reveals the special rhythms and character of St. Martin. The cuisine of St. Martin represents the fusion of these tropical ingredients with African and French cooking traditions.

JUNE KELLY

Introduction

My name is Jeanne Louise Duzant Chance. My friends call me "Modie" because my son called me that when, as a small child, he couldn't say "Mother." Many years ago I was given the name "Ma Chance," short for Madame Chance, by visiting Americans. I was born in the village of Grand Case, St. Martin, in 1910 and have lived here my entire life. I have two older sisters. My father died when I was about five, and my older sisters supported my mother and me. Although we had very little money, our home was filled with love. My husband, Leon Chance, was also born in Grand Case. We have one son, a granddaughter and a grandson, one adopted grandson, and two great-grandchildren. All live here except our granddaughter, who is in Paris taking her law examinations. My parents, Eliza and Charles Duzant, and my husband's parents were born in Grand Case. That makes five generations of our family born and raised here.

I have never had a desire to live anyplace besides St. Martin, where life has been so good to me. Grand Case Bay is about fifty feet from my door with its beautiful blue waters. At night we can see the lights of Anguilla across the bay. On our property we have many plants and trees—breadfruit, mango, papaya, almond. My husband, Chancy, loves plants of all kinds and they grow beautifully under his care. In front of our home we have an evergreen tree that we decorate with lights at Christmastime. I get great pleasure from my adopted grandson, Mark, who is twelve and lives with Chancy and me, and from my great-granddaughters, Alyssa and Shauntée, who are just starting school. They visit me every day. Life for me now is much quieter. Much of my time I spend on our porch enjoying my family and friends.

When I was a young child, I would watch my mother cooking,

but it wasn't until my teens that I had a desire to cook. I best enjoyed sports, music, and dance, and when I was thirteen years old I began to take violin lessons. There was no one in Grand Case to teach music, so I walked to Marigot three days a week for my lessons. I would leave for Marigot about eight o'clock in the morning and return home at noon. When I arrived home, I would eat the lunch my mother had prepared. After resting, I would work on handicraft that I was preparing for my hope chest. I made doilies, dresses, pillowcases, and sheets. I still have one of the sheets that I made. My mother worked very hard and she spent much time and energy taking care of the sick. So to help her, I began cooking. Many of the recipes I now cook are my mother's. As I watched, she would show me what she was doing and tell me what she had learned from her mother. Sometimes I would make changes in the dishes she taught me or I would experiment and make up my own. From the very beginning I liked to cook. The first things I learned to cook were stew meats, stew fish, calaloo soup, stewed peas, custard cakes, and candies.

In December 1933 I married Leon Chance (our friends call him "Chancy"). After we were married and had our son, I really began to get pleasure from cooking. That was probably because my husband and son enjoyed my food so much. And other people enjoyed my cooking too. Cooking became my pastime. All day long people could smell the tempting aromas from my kitchen.

I became a professional cook when I was in my early twenties. My husband had a business and I would cook dinner for the customers several nights a week. We served the food in our garden on tables arranged around a beautiful almond tree with colored lights hanging from it. Sometimes we would have as many as fifty people. That was the beginning.

During this time I also began baking and selling bread, sweet cakes, pies, coconut candies, pastries, and patties. The bread was shaped into long loaves and baked in an outdoor oven made from bricks and white lime, which had been heated by burning wood inside it. In the morning, after everything was baked, the young women who helped me would set up stands on the road and go out and sell the food. Others would take trays with rice, sugar, and flour packed by the pound and go all over the island to sell—to Marigot, Savannah, Cul de Sac, and the French Quarter.

When tourism began in St. Martin and the visitors asked for a restaurant with creole food, my friends told them to call Ma Chance, the best cook on the island. I really didn't have a restaurant then, but that's how the business started. There was no publicity, just word of mouth, one person telling another.

Around 1935 Leon and I had an extra room built on the front of our house and opened our restaurant called "Ma Chance's Hide-Out." There weren't any other restaurants in Grand Case, nor even in Marigot.

I kept Ma Chance's Hide-Out until the mid-1950s when I retired. Some people say that I am the most "retiring woman" on St. Martin. I keep retiring and then start working again.

After I moved from Ma Chance's Hide-Out people followed me here, and so I started cooking in my new house and serving home-style dinners. Guests make reservations in advance. Usually I serve about eight to ten people, but sometimes we have many more. My home-style restaurant is the best. People feel at ease and enjoy the relaxed atmosphere. My business got a big boost in the mid-1960s when some very generous comments were made about my restaurant in the Fielding's travel guide about the Caribbean islands.

My son operated Ma Chance's Hide-Out for a while after I left, and then Christophine, my adopted daughter, ran her restaurant there until 1981. She renamed it "Chez Christophine," and it became quite famous. There was even a table wine made in France that was labeled "Chez Christophine."

Christophine's booth at the holiday festivals was always the best. She would tell everyone that she had learned her cooking touch from Ma Chance. She would have conch and dumplings, whelks (periwinkles), turtle steaks, red snapper, coconut pie, sweet potato pie, and many other wonderful things.

Christophine had been five years old when she told her mother that she wanted to come and live with me. We were very close. When she died in 1981, it was as if half my life went out of me.

Most of my assistants have stayed with me for many years. We have become very attached—like family. Others started their own restaurants on St. Martin, on other islands, and in the United States. Now I have Nine and Marie who help me cook. Claire and Clemencia, who are from Grand Case and are my very good friends, do the serving.

THE OLD DAYS

In the olden days there were many fishermen on St. Martin and often their catch was given away. My son had a boat, *The Patricia,* named after my granddaughter. Some nights he would catch as many as twelve kingfish and give them to our friends. Today we have very few fishermen, some in Marigot but few in Grand Case. Although there are all kinds of fish in the waters around St. Martin—kingfish, red snapper, blackfish, goatfish, grouper, yellowtail, bonito—fish is still very scarce. Fishing now has become an industry and the fish are expensive.

Before tourism came, people used to work very hard in the cotton fields and the salt fields. They had large farms, grew sugar cane, and made syrup. At that time we grew all our own vegetables and fruits—breadfruits, tannia seeds, plantains, pumpkins (winter squash), christophenes, eggplant, soursops, prickly pears, tamarinds, mangoes, guavas, guavaberries, gooseberries, plums, cherries, papayas, sugar apples.

Now few people do any farming. Some may have a small plot, but all the produce for sale is imported from Guadeloupe, Dominica, St. Kitts, and other islands. People stopped doing large-scale farming on St. Martin about twenty years ago. The island was very dry, little rain fell, and people tired of planting and not reaping any crops. About this time tourism started to grow and become more important to the island. More and more people moved from farming and turned to tourism to find their livelihoods.

COOKING ON THE ISLAND

In Grand Case, the food is simple. The women take great pride in their French creole cooking. It is the mixture of ingredients that makes it special. I use basic utensils: heavy skillets and heavy pots. Everything is prepared very much as I learned from my mother, although sometimes I use an electric mixer or blender or pressure cooker.

In the olden days, all the food was fresh, and I still use fresh food in my cooking. People used to live so long, many into their nineties, because they got everything directly from the earth or from the sea—fresh fish, fresh vegetables just picked, all the juices running out.

Many times people did not even wash or peel the vegetables. They had potatoes that they called "sand-a-ground potatoes" because they were dug from the sand. They were like sweet potatoes but smaller, and they were cooked by the basketful with the skins on and served with roast fish and a dip made from lemon juice, a little oil, pepper, a little salt, and water. And in those days people drank a lot of milk. For breakfast, instead of having bread, they would have boiled potatoes with milk. Their lunch would be fish, cornmeal, and stewed peas. For dinner there would be fried fish, soup, and dessert. Those were typical meals. For snacks, there would be cassava bread and milk.

Have you ever heard of cassava bread? It has always been a favorite on St. Martin. Cassava is a root vegetable, and the skin, which we call the husk, is used to make bread. In the olden days, when the houses were made of thatch, people would put the husks on the roof of their house to dry. The bread is crispy and is delicious to eat with fish or soup or just a glass of milk.

Starch was made from the flesh of the cassava. The flesh was washed, dried, and grated and wrapped in a cloth. The liquid was squeezed out and caught in a vessel. Starch formed at the bottom of the liquid and was put in the sun to dry and then used to stiffen clothes. The shirt collars and cuffs would look so good that people called the men who wore them "swagger boys."

Corn was another crop that we used a lot. In the old system of pounding corn—used before my time—people made a huge mortar and pestle from the trunk of a tree. The inside of the trunk was cut out to form the rounded vessel, which was polished well. The pestle was made from a tree branch. The corn was placed in the mortar and pounded fine to make cornmeal for dumplings, porridge, pudding, or kenkies.

I have a tree-trunk mortar and pestle on my porch. Many tourists ask if they could buy it, but I wouldn't sell it for any amount of money. I love it because it is part of the history of St. Martin and is a remembrance of the older generation.

There have been a lot of changes in Grand Case since my young days. Back then, Grand Case was a peaceful little village. The main street was six feet wide, and when my friends and I were walking along holding hands, we would have to let go so that other people could pass by.

Today there is no more walking. Cars take us wherever we want to go. The main street is sixteen feet wide. The traffic is amazing, with all kinds of cars, trucks, bicycles, motorcycles. The main street where I live is so crowded with restaurants and with cars coming and going that we often have traffic jams. A policeman has to direct the traffic on Friday and Saturday nights.

Most people go to the market in Marigot to buy their produce. The market is open from Monday to Saturday, but Saturday is the biggest shopping day. Boats come from the other islands and meet in Marigot, bringing people to shop in the market and also bringing food and other goods to be sold.

About seven years ago I decided to write a cookbook because many of my guests asked me for recipes so they could cook the dishes they had eaten. Writing a cookbook allowed me to pass on the dishes I learned from my mother so everybody could enjoy them. I have added many of my own recipes also, but basically the dishes are the early creole cooking of St. Martin, a combination of French and native cooking using the fish, poultry, vegetables, and fruits indigenous to the island. I am happy that others will be able to enjoy the foods I have been cooking for more than fifty years.

MA CHANCE

A Note on Cooking Temperatures

All cooking temperatures are given in degrees Fahrenheit. A conversion table is provided below for those cooking in degrees Celsius.

Fahrenheit	Celsius
225°	107°
230°	110°
250°	121°
275°	135°
300°	149°
325°	163°
350°	177°
360°	182°
375°	190°
400°	204°
425°	218°
450°	232°

Appetizers

Codfish Fritters

My fritters are delicious. They can be served as appetizers, or as part of the main course, or as a fine luncheon dish with a green salad.

1/2 pound salt codfish
2 tablespoons butter
1 tablespoon olive oil
1 large onion, chopped
1 stalk celery, chopped
1/2 green pepper, chopped
1 large tomato, chopped
1 teaspoon crushed thyme

4 drops Tabasco
1/4 teaspoon pepper
1 cup flour
1 teaspoon baking powder
3 egg yolks, beaten
1 1/2 cups milk
corn oil for deep frying

To remove salt, soak codfish in cold water for 12 hours. Drain. Boil in water to cover for 5 minutes. Drain. Remove bones and mince.

In a heavy skillet, heat butter and olive oil over a moderate flame, and sauté onion, celery, and green pepper until vegetables are tender. Remove vegetables with a slotted spoon and pour off grease. In a separate bowl, thoroughly mix vegetables, tomato, thyme, Tabasco, pepper, and codfish.

In a mixing bowl, sift together flour and baking powder. Add egg yolks and milk and mix until thoroughly blended. Add to vegetable and codfish mixture and blend. In a heavy skillet, heat the corn oil (360°). Drop 2 tablespoons of mixture at a time in hot oil. Deep fry until golden brown, about 6 minutes. Remove fritters with a slotted spoon or strainer and drain on paper towel. Serve hot. *Serves about 6; makes about 12 fritters.*

Tannia Seed Fritters

Tannia seed is also known as tanier, tanyah, yautia, malanga, and ocumo. The tannia seed is a root vegetable that is a member of the yam family. The outer skin is brown, similar in color and texture to a thin coconut skin. The pulp is coarsely textured and is a white to orange-rose or purplish color.

*1/2 pound tannia seed, peeled
  and grated*
*1/4 pound pumpkin (winter
  squash), peeled and grated*
1 onion, grated
1/4 cup flour
1/4 teaspoon baking powder
2 egg yolks, lightly beaten

2 tablespoons butter, melted
2 tablespoons milk
3 drops Tabasco
1/4 teaspoon thyme, crushed
salt to taste
pepper to taste
corn oil for deep frying

Mix tannia seed, pumpkin, and onion in a bowl. Sift together flour and baking powder and add to bowl. Add all other ingredients *except* oil and blend until smooth.

Heat oil in a heavy skillet. Drop 1 tablespoon of mixture at a time in hot oil, cooking until golden brown on each side, about 3 minutes. Remove fritters with a slotted spoon or strainer and place on paper towel to remove excess oil. Serve warm. *Serves about 12; makes about 18 fritters.*

Breadfruit Fritters

Breadfruits grow on large, beautiful trees that were introduced to the West Indies from the South Pacific in 1792 by Captain Bligh. I have a breadfruit tree in my backyard. The fruit usually grows to about 4 to 8 inches in diameter. The skin is green, and the flesh is a yellowish white. Although in tropical countries it is possible to buy the exact amount of breadfruit needed for a particular recipe, in nontropical countries it is usually necessary to buy an entire breadfruit.

1 ripe medium breadfruit
1/4 cup flour
1/4 teaspoon baking powder
dash of salt

2 egg yolks, lightly beaten
1/2 cup milk
corn oil for deep frying

Cut breadfruit in quarters, peel, and cook in salted boiling water to cover for 20 minutes. Drain, cool, and puree or mash.

Sift together flour, baking powder, and salt. Combine egg yolks, milk, and breadfruit. Add to flour mixture and stir until well blended.

Heat oil in a heavy skillet. Drop 1 tablespoon of mixture at a time in hot oil (375°), cooking until golden brown on each side, 3 to 4 minutes. Remove fritters with a slotted spoon or strainer. Place on paper towel to remove excess oil. Serve warm. *Serves 10; makes about 18 fritters.*

Pumpkin Fritters

1/2 pound pumpkin, peeled and
   cut into quarters
2 tablespoons flour
1 teaspoon baking powder
3 tablespoons sugar
1/4 teaspoon nutmeg

2 egg yolks, lightly beaten
3 tablespoons milk
2 tablespoons butter, melted
1 teaspoon vanilla extract
corn oil for frying

Put pumpkin in boiling water to cover. Boil until soft, about 10 minutes. Mash.

Sift together flour, baking powder, sugar, and nutmeg in a mixing bowl. Blend in all remaining ingredients *except* oil and stir until smooth.

Heat oil in a heavy skillet. Drop 1 tablespoon of mixture at a time in hot oil, cooking until golden brown on each side, about 3 minutes. Remove fritters with a slotted spoon or strainer and place on paper towel to remove excess oil. Serve warm. *Serves about 10; makes about 20 fritters.*

NOTE: Winter squash, such as Hubbard, acorn, or butternut squash, may be substituted for the pumpkin.

Banana Fritters

2 cups flour
1 teaspoon baking powder
1/4 teaspoon salt
2 tablespoons sugar (or to taste)
1/4 teaspoon cinnamon
4 large ripe bananas, mashed or
  lightly pureed

2 egg yolks, lightly beaten
1/2 cup milk
2 tablespoons butter, melted
1 teaspoon vanilla extract
1 tablespoon rum
corn oil for deep frying

In a mixing bowl, sift together flour, baking powder, salt, sugar, and cinnamon. Blend in all remaining ingredients *except* oil and stir until smooth.

Heat oil in a heavy skillet. Drop about 1 tablespoon of mixture at a time into hot oil, cooking until golden brown on each side, about 3 to 4 minutes. Remove fritters with a slotted spoon or strainer and place on paper towel to remove excess oil. Serve warm. *Serves 10; makes about 18 fritters.*

Oyster Cornmeal Fritters

2 cups canned oysters, or 3 to
  3 1/2 cups fresh shucked oysters
1 cup pancake mix (see recipe
  below)

2 tablespoons cornmeal
1 teaspoon salt
1/4 teaspoon ground pepper
3/4 cup corn oil

Drain oysters, reserving liquid. Mix pancake mix, cornmeal, salt, and pepper. Gently fold in oysters. The batter must be thick. If it is too thick, add oyster liquid by the tablespoon until you get the desired consistency—that of heavy cream.

Heat oil in a medium-sized heavy skillet. Drop in about 2 table-spoons of batter at a time. Make sure to include at least 2 oysters in each portion. Cook until golden brown on one side, 1 or 2 minutes, then turn carefully and brown on other side. Remove fritters with a slotted spoon or strainer and place on paper towel to remove excess oil. *Makes about 10 fritters.*

PANCAKE MIX

1 1/4 cups flour
3 teaspoons baking powder
1/2 teaspoon salt

1 tablespoon sugar
1 cup milk
1 egg, beaten

Sift together dry ingredients. Add milk and egg. Stir briefly but vigorously. *Makes about 2 cups.*

Crab Fritters

1 cup crabmeat, or 6 to 8 crabs
1 onion, chopped
1 carrot, grated
1 egg
1/2 cup milk
1 cup flour
1/2 teaspoon baking powder
1/2 teaspoon sugar

pinch of salt
pepper to taste
juice of 1 lemon
1 teaspoon fresh garlic, chopped
1 teaspoon fresh parsley, chopped
1/4 teaspoon Worcestershire sauce
corn oil for frying

Prepare crabs according to the method on page 76.

In a mixing bowl, beat egg, add milk, and stir. Sift together dry ingredients and add to egg and milk mixture. Blend well. Add all remaining ingredients except oil and mix gently. Fold in crabmeat.

Heat oil in a large heavy skillet. Drop mixture into hot oil, 1 tablespoon at a time, and fry until golden brown on both sides. With a slotted spoon, remove fritters and drain on paper towel. *Serves about 8; makes about 16 fritters.*

Beef Patties

Patties are plump little pastries filled with spicy meat, shrimp, or fish. They are served everywhere around the world at tea or cocktail parties as appetizers or with the main course. Patties should be prepared in abundance, since they disappear quickly. They can be baked or deep fried, served hot or cold. I prefer them deep fried and served hot.

MEAT FILLING
1 pound lean ground beef
2 medium onions, minced
1 large green pepper, minced
1 clove garlic, minced
1 hot red pepper, minced
salt and pepper to taste
2 tablespoons olive oil
2 eggs

CRUST
1 egg
14 tablespoons shortening
1/2 teaspoon salt
2 1/2 cups flour
5 to 6 tablespoons ice water

To prepare meat filling: Mix all ingredients *except* eggs in a heavy pot. Cook over medium heat until meat loses its color, about 5 to 7 minutes. Remove from heat. Pour off grease. Place in a bowl and cool slightly. Beat eggs and add to mixture. Mix thoroughly.

To prepare crust: Separate egg. Beat white lightly. Hold yolk. (Although the entire egg can be used in the crust if desired, I prefer to use the white only.) Fold shortening and salt into the egg white. Add flour, a little at a time. Add water and remaining flour until flour is completely absorbed.

After dough is formed, knead well. With a floured rolling pin, roll dough into a thin sheet, then cut out circles about 3 inches in diameter. Place 1 tablespoon of filling in the center of each pastry circle. Moisten edges of pattie with reserved egg yolk and fold pastry circle over on itself. Press edges firmly. Prick patties with a fork and fry in deep hot oil (375°) until golden brown. If baking, place patties on a greased cookie sheet and bake in preheated 400° oven until golden brown on both sides. *Makes about 1 1/2 dozen.*

NOTE: Patties may be prepared in advance and reheated in oven about 5 minutes before serving.

Salt Codfish Patties

FISH FILLING
1 *pound salt codfish*
2 *medium onions, sliced*
1 *large green pepper, minced*
2 *tablespoons olive oil*
salt to taste
freshly ground pepper to taste
3 *drops Tabasco (or to taste)*
1 *egg, beaten*
1 *to 2 tablespoons milk (if*
   needed)

CRUST
1 *egg*
14 *tablespoons shortening*
1/2 teaspoon salt
21/2 cups flour
5 *to 6 tablespoons ice water*

To prepare fish filling: To remove salt, soak codfish in cold water for 12 hours. Drain. Boil in water to cover for 3 to 4 minutes. Drain. Remove bones and mince. In a skillet, sauté onions and green pepper in oil over moderate heat until onions are tender. Add minced codfish and stir for about 3 minutes. Drain off as much oil as possible. In a bowl, add salt, pepper, and Tabasco to sautéed mixture. Fold in beaten egg and mix thoroughly. If mixture seems dry, add 1 to 2 tablespoons of milk.

To prepare crust: Separate egg. Beat white lightly. Hold yolk. (Although the entire egg can be used in the crust if desired, I prefer to use the white only.) Fold shortening and salt into the egg white. Add flour, a little at a time. Add water and remaining flour until flour is completely absorbed.

After dough is formed, knead well. With a floured rolling pin, roll dough into a thin sheet, then cut out circles about 3 inches in diameter. Place 1 tablespoon of filling in the center of each pastry circle. Moisten edges of pattie with reserved egg yolk and fold pastry circle over on itself. Press edges firmly. Prick patties with a fork and fry in deep hot oil (375°) until golden brown. If baking, place patties on a greased cookie sheet and bake in preheated 400° oven until golden brown on both sides. *Makes about 1 1/2 dozen.*

NOTE: Patties may be prepared in advance and reheated in oven about 5 minutes before serving.

Oysters à la King

3 slices bacon
1 small onion, chopped
1 small stalk celery, chopped
1 teaspoon lime juice
1 to 2 tablespoons oyster liquid
1 teaspoon salt

1/2 teaspoon pepper
1/4 teaspoon Worcestershire sauce
3 drops cayenne sauce
2 dozen fresh oysters, or 2 cups
    canned oysters
6 pieces buttered toast

Preheat oven to 400°.

Fry bacon in a heavy skillet until crisp. Remove bacon from skillet and crumble. Set aside. Pour off most of the grease from skillet. Sauté onion and celery in skillet until tender. Mix in lime juice, oyster liquid, seasonings, Worcestershire sauce, and cayenne sauce. Add bacon.

Drain oysters and arrange in a single layer in a shallow baking pan. Spread mixture over oysters. Bake for 10 to 15 minutes. Serve on buttered toast. *Serves 6.*

Oysters in Vinegar Sauce

1 cup red wine vinegar
1 clove garlic, minced
1 medium onion, chopped or
    thinly sliced
salt and freshly ground pepper
    to taste

1 dozen fresh oysters
lettuce leaves

GARNISH
sliced tomatoes
sliced avocado

In a small bowl, mix vinegar, garlic, onion, and seasonings together. Marinate 2 to 3 hours at room temperature.

Boil oysters in shell until they open. As shells open, remove from pot and drain in colander. When cool enough to handle, remove oysters from shell. Serve on a bed of lettuce leaves, garnish with sliced tomatoes and sliced avocado and sauce for dipping. *Serves 4 to 6.*

Stuffed Clams

Stuffed clams can be served either warm or cold.

12 medium cherrystone clams
1/4 teaspoon lemon juice
salt and pepper to taste
1 clove garlic, chopped
4 drops Tabasco, or 2 dashes of
  cayenne sauce

1/2 cup water
1/4 cup butter, melted
1 cup breadcrumbs
1 teaspoon crushed parsley flakes
paprika
1 lemon, cut into wedges

Preheat oven to 400°.

Scrub clams with a stiff brush under cold running water. Wash in several waters. Place clams close together in the top of a steamer and sprinkle with lemon juice, salt, pepper, garlic, and Tabasco. Place water in the bottom of the steamer. Cover the pot and steam over moderate heat until shells open, no longer than 10 minutes. Remove clams.

Strain clam broth through cheesecloth and reserve. Grind or finely chop clams, mix well with butter, breadcrumbs, and parsley. If mixture is too dry, moisten with some reserved liquid.

Fill shells with mixture and place in a baking pan. Sprinkle tops lightly and evenly with paprika. Bake clams until bubbly, about 10 to 15 minutes. Serve with lemon wedges. *Serves 3 or 4.*

Stuffed Escargots

Cleaning and preparing fresh escargots takes so much time that many people prefer to buy them canned and ready to cook. The shells are usually sold separately.

1/2 cup unsalted butter
1 1/2 tablespoons fresh parsley,
  finely chopped
1 1/2 tablespoons onion, minced
1 to 2 tablespoons celery, minced

1 tablespoon crushed garlic
1/4 teaspoon salt
ground pepper to taste
2 dozen canned escargots and
  shells

Preheat oven to 425°.

Cream butter until soft and add parsley, onion, celery, garlic, salt, and pepper. Stuff shells with a little of the mixture. Add one escargot per shell. Arrange shells in a shallow baking pan sprinkled with water. Bake in oven for 5 minutes. *Serves 2 to 4.*

Salt Codfish Balls

This delicious dish can be used as an appetizer or snack, or can be served with the main course.

1/2 pound salt codfish
2 medium white potatoes, peeled
* and cut in half*
1/4 pound pumpkin (winter
* squash), peeled and cut in*
* pieces*
2 egg yolks
1 large onion, chopped
1 stalk celery, chopped

1/2 green pepper, seeded
* and chopped*
2 tablespoons butter
4 tablespoons flour
1 tablespoon baking powder
1/4 teaspoon salt
1/2 teaspoon pepper
1/2 teaspoon thyme
corn oil for deep frying

To remove salt, soak codfish in water for 12 hours. Drain. Place in boiling water and simmer for 5 minutes. Drain and shred codfish.

Boil potatoes and pumpkin until potatoes are tender when pricked with a fork. Drain. Mash. Combine codfish and mashed ingredients. Add egg yolks, one at a time. Blend well.

In a heavy skillet, sauté over moderate heat onion, celery, and green pepper in 1 tablespoon of butter. In a large bowl, sift flour, baking powder, salt, and pepper. Add to dry ingredients fish mixture, sautéed vegetables, 1 tablespoon of butter, and thyme. Blend well.

Lightly coat the palms of your hands with flour and shape the mixture into balls about 2 inches in diameter. In a heavy skillet, deep fry the balls in hot oil (375°) until golden brown, about 10 minutes. Drain on paper towel to remove excess oil and serve. *Serves 4 to 6; makes about 8 balls.*

Avocado Dip

1 clove garlic
2 ripe avocados
juice of 2 limes
1 medium onion, chopped
1 medium tomato, chopped
1 medium green pepper, chopped
1 tablespoon fresh coriander
  leaves, minced

1 teaspoon fresh parsley, chopped
pinch of oregano
salt to taste
freshly ground pepper to taste
1 tablespoon olive oil
dash of hot sauce
1 tablespoon grated cheese

Wipe inside of a bowl with garlic clove. Peel and pit avocados. Mash avocado with a fork or potato masher. Add lime juice and blend. Add onion, tomato, green pepper, and seasonings and blend. Chill. Place 1 avocado pit in mixture to keep it green. Add olive oil, hot sauce, and grated cheese and blend just before serving. *Serves 6.*

Crabmeat-Stuffed Eggs

1 cup crabmeat, or 6 to 8 crabs
1 onion
1 carrot
12 hard-boiled eggs
1 stalk celery, minced
2 tablespoons mayonnaise

1 teaspoon fresh garlic, chopped
1/2 teaspoon fresh parsley, chopped
1/4 teaspoon salt
pepper to taste
1 teaspoon dry mustard
Tabasco to taste

Prepare crabs according to the method on page 76. Mince crabmeat and set aside.

Peel eggs and cut in half lengthwise. Remove yolks. Mash yolks well in a bowl. Add celery, mayonnaise, seasonings, Tabasco, and crabmeat. Mix well. Stuff eggs. Chill before serving. *Serves 12.*

Crab Dip

1 dozen crabs (6 claws per
  person)
2 small onions, one whole and
  one thinly sliced
1 carrot
1 tomato, thinly sliced

1 tablespoon red wine vinegar
2 tablespoons olive oil
1 tablespoon corn oil
pinch of salt and pepper
2 tablespoons fresh basil, chopped

Cook crabs according to the method on page 76. Remove claws. When claws are cool enough to handle, arrange them on a serving platter with sliced onion and tomato.

In a bowl, mix together vinegar, olive oil, corn oil, salt, and pepper. Spoon sauce over tomato, onion, and crab claws. Sprinkle with chopped basil. *Serves 4.*

NOTE: The crab bodies should be reserved for the stuffed-crab recipes in this book.

Ma Chance's Hot Pepper Sauce

This sauce can be used in any recipe calling for hot sauce or to spice up any dish. But take some words of warning: Use with caution!

12 fresh yellow or red hot
   peppers, seeded and finely
   chopped (see Note below)
6 cloves garlic, minced
1 large onion, minced

6 cloves, crushed
1/4 teaspoon salt
1 cup vinegar
1 cup water
2 tablespoons vegetable oil

Place peppers in a quart jar. Add all remaining ingredients *except* oil. Shake well. Pour oil on top and let stand for 2 hours. Shake well before using.

This sauce can be used immediately or kept indefinitely. Use it with meat or fish recipes to taste.

NOTE: Wash your hands immediately after handling the hot peppers.

Soups

My soups are hearty, tangy dishes that are easy to prepare and may be served with johnnycakes (see recipes on pp. 121–122).

In general, the flavor of soups benefits if the soups stand for several hours and are then reheated before serving, liquid being added if necessary.

Ma Chance's Creole Soup

1 pound dried green peas
8 cups cold water
1 teaspoon fresh thyme
1/4 cup fresh parsley, chopped
1 teaspoon sugar
2 bay leaves
1/2 pound salt pork, cut into
  1/4-inch cubes
1 large onion, chopped

2 cloves garlic, minced
1 stalk celery with leaves,
  chopped
1 large sweet potato, peeled
  and chopped
1/4 pound pumpkin (winter
  squash), peeled and chopped
salt and freshly ground pepper
  to taste

Soak dried green peas overnight in cold water to cover. Drain. In a large soup kettle, combine peas, water, thyme, parsley, sugar, and bay leaves. Set aside.

In a small skillet, fry the salt pork until crisp. With a slotted spoon, remove from skillet and add to soup kettle. In the same skillet, sauté onion, garlic, and celery for about 5 minutes, or until onion is tender. With a slotted spoon, remove vegetables from skillet and add to soup kettle.

Bring water to a boil. Reduce heat and simmer covered for 2 hours. Add sweet potato and pumpkin. Cover and simmer for an additional 30 minutes, or until vegetables are tender. It may be necessary to add more water if soup becomes too thick. Season with salt and pepper. *Serves 6.*

NOTE: Ham hocks may be substituted for salt pork.

Pigeon Peas Soup

Pigeon peas are tan or light brown with a black "eye" and are available dried in most food stores. They are also known as cajanus, gongo peas, and gandules.

1 pound dried pigeon peas
1/4 pound salt pork, diced
6 cups water
1 medium onion, sliced
1 clove garlic, minced
1 stalk celery with leaves, diced
1/2 cup carrots, diced

1/4 teaspoon thyme
1/2 teaspoon oregano
2 cups chicken broth
1/4 teaspoon freshly ground pepper
salt to taste
1 bay leaf

Soak peas in 3 to 4 cups of cold water overnight. Drain and rinse peas.

Blanch salt pork in boiling water for 10 minutes. Drain. In a soup kettle, cook salt pork over low heat for 5 minutes. Add peas, water, and all remaining ingredients. Bring to a boil, cover, and simmer 2 to 3 hours, or until the peas are tender. Remove bay leaf. Correct seasoning. *Serves 6.*

NOTE: Ham hocks may be substituted for salt pork.

Calaloo Soup with Dumplings

Calaloo is probably one of the most popular soups in the Caribbean. If you can't find calaloo, you can use spinach, watercress, young kale, or Swiss chard.

1 pound calaloo with stems,
  finely chopped
3/4 pound salt pork, cut into
  1/4-inch cubes
1 large onion, chopped
2 cloves garlic, minced
1 stalk celery with leaves,
  chopped
1 gallon water

1 teaspoon cayenne
1/4 teaspoon fresh thyme, crushed
1 tablespoon tomato paste
2 medium sweet potatoes, peeled
  and sliced
1/4 pound pumpkin (winter
  squash), peeled and sliced
salt and pepper to taste
dumplings (see recipe below)

Wash calaloo thoroughly. In a large skillet, fry the salt pork until crisp. With a slotted spoon, remove from skillet and place in a soup kettle.

In the same skillet, sauté onion, garlic, and celery for about 5 minutes, or until onion is tender. With a slotted spoon, remove vegetables from skillet and add to soup kettle. Add calaloo and all remaining ingredients *except* salt and pepper and dumplings. Bring water to a boil. Reduce heat and simmer covered for 45 minutes. Season with salt and pepper.

Turn off heat and let ingredients sit for at least 1 hour. Reheat to simmer just before serving. Add dumplings, cover tightly, and simmer for 15 minutes. *Serves 8.*

NOTE: Smoked turkey or a ham bone can be substituted for the salt pork.

DUMPLINGS

1 cup flour
1/4 cup cornmeal
2 teaspoons baking powder
1/2 teaspoon salt
1/4 teaspoon cinnamon

1 teaspoon sugar
1 egg
1/2 cup milk
2 tablespoons butter, melted

In a mixing bowl, sift together flour, cornmeal, baking powder, salt, cinnamon, and sugar. In a separate bowl, combine egg, milk, and butter. Slowly add liquid to dry ingredients, stirring until batter is moistened.

Work dough with your fingers until it is stiff and sticks together. Cover with a linen towel and let stand for 5 minutes. Roll dough into a long roll about 1½ inches in diameter, or larger if desired. Cut into diagonal strips about 1 inch wide. Mold each strip with fingers into an oval shape. *Makes about 15 dumplings.*

Peanut Soup

Long ago, peanuts were pounded by mortar and pestle to make this soup. Today, peanut butter makes the soup much easier to prepare. Peanut soup is an excellent first course, but it is rich and only small portions, about 1 cup per person, are recommended.

½ cup peanut butter, or 1 cup
  unsalted dry-roasted peanuts,
  crushed
2 cups chicken broth

½ small onion, finely grated
dash of Tabasco
salt to taste
1 cup milk

Place peanut butter in a pot over low heat and gradually whisk in 1 cup chicken broth. Simmer slowly for 10 minutes. Stir in onion, Tabasco, and salt. Simmer slowly for 10 minutes more, stirring occasionally. Stir in milk and second cup of broth, bring to a slow simmer again, stir until mixture is smooth and creamy. If soup is too thick, add more milk and adjust seasoning. If it is too thin, blend in more peanut butter, 1 tablespoon at a time. *Serves 4.*

Fish Soup

2 pounds fish (whitefish, haddock,
   halibut, or other firm, mild,
   lean fish), cleaned and scaled
1 clove garlic, crushed
salt to taste
pepper to taste
2 tablespoons olive oil
1 tablespoon butter
1 large onion, chopped
1/2 green pepper, chopped
1 hot red pepper, seeded and
   chopped

4 cups water
4 carrots, chopped
4 white potatoes, peeled and
   chopped
1 teaspoon tomato paste
1/4 teaspoon crushed thyme
1 tablespoon crushed parsley
3 cloves, crushed
corn oil for frying

Remove skin from fish and cut into 2-inch pieces. Season with garlic, salt, and pepper. Marinate for 30 minutes.

In a heavy pot, heat oil and butter over a moderate flame and sauté onion, green pepper, and red pepper until onion is tender. Add water, carrots, potatoes, tomato paste, thyme, parsley, and cloves. Bring water to a boil, reduce heat, and simmer uncovered for 30 minutes. Stir occasionally.

While vegetables are simmering, deep fry fish in hot oil (350°) for 5 minutes. Drain on paper towel. Remove bones from fish and add fish to soup. Simmer slowly uncovered for 5 to 7 minutes. *Serves 6.*

Ma Chance's Fish Chowder

1/4 pound salt pork, diced
1/2 cup celery, chopped
1 large onion, chopped
1/2 teaspoon thyme
1 bay leaf
5 cups cold water
2 cups diced potatoes
2 pounds fish fillet (whitefish,
  halibut, haddock, cod), cut into
  1-inch cubes

1 cup milk
1 cup heavy cream
2 tablespoons flour
1/8 teaspoon cayenne pepper
salt and white pepper to taste
1 tablespoon fresh parsley,
  minced

Blanch salt pork in boiling water for 10 minutes. Drain. In a heavy soup kettle, fry salt pork over low heat for 5 minutes. Add celery and onion and sauté until tender. Add thyme, bay leaf, water, and potatoes. Bring to a boil. Reduce heat. Simmer covered for 15 to 20 minutes, or until potatoes are tender.

In a separate bowl, blend thoroughly milk, cream, and flour. Add to soup slowly. Simmer, stirring constantly, until soup thickens, 10 to 15 minutes. Add fish and simmer 5 minutes. Season with cayenne, salt, and pepper. Garnish with parsley. *Serves 8.*

NOTE: Chowder can be served immediately or cooled to room temperature and refrigerated until ready to use. Before reheating, remove fish from chowder and set aside. Bring liquid to a simmer. Then add fish, stir, heat, garnish, and serve.

Turtle Soup

3 quarts water
1 pound turtle stew meat, cut
 into medium-sized pieces
2 onions, chopped
1 stalk celery, chopped
1/4 teaspoon thyme
1 clove garlic, minced
1 tablespoon parsley
1 bay leaf
1/2 teaspoon salt
1/4 teaspoon freshly ground black
 pepper

1/2 red pepper, chopped
2 medium white potatoes, peeled
 and cubed
2 carrots, coarsely chopped
1 tablespoon tomato paste
1 tablespoon olive oil
1/4 pound vermicelli, broken into
 small pieces
1/4 cup red wine or sherry

In a heavy pot with 3 quarts of water, place turtle meat, onions, celery, thyme, garlic, parsley, bay leaf, salt, and pepper. Simmer for 2 hours. Add all remaining ingredients *except* wine and vermicelli. Simmer for another 2 hours. Add vermicelli and wine and simmer for 10 minutes. Remove from heat, stir, and let stand for 15 minutes before serving. Remove bay leaf. *Serves 6.*

Conch Soup

The conch is a large shellfish. Its flesh is white but becomes a grayish putty color after boiling.

To prepare the conch meat: Wash thoroughly in water and then rub all over with lime juice to remove the slick coating that covers the flesh. Pound with a mallet to tenderize it, then marinate for 2 hours in lime juice. After trimming the edges, put in boiling water and boil for 10 minutes to remove sweet taste.

1 pound conch meat	1 1/2 quarts chicken broth
juice of 2 limes	1 medium tomato, cut in half
2 quarts water	1 carrot, chopped
1 tablespoon olive oil	1/2 teaspoon crushed thyme
1 tablespoon butter	1/8 pound vermicelli, broken into
1 green pepper, sliced	small pieces
2 cloves garlic, crushed	salt and white pepper to taste
1 large onion, sliced	1/4 cup fresh parsley, chopped

Prepare conch according to the directions above. Cut into bite-sized pieces. Add to 2 quarts of boiling water in pressure cooker. Cover pressure cooker and cook for 30 minutes. Remove pressure cooker from heat and let pressure drop, or put pot under cold running water. When pressure drops, remove top.

Heat oil and butter in a heavy pot over a moderate flame, and sauté conch, green pepper, garlic, and onion until conch is golden. Add chicken broth, tomato, carrot, and thyme. Cover and simmer until conch is tender, about 1 1/2 hours. Add vermicelli and simmer for 10 minutes, or until vermicelli are soft. Season to taste with salt and pepper. Remove from heat and let stand covered for 3 to 4 hours. Reheat and sprinkle with parsley immediately before serving. *Serves 8.*

Chicken Chow Soup

This dish is so simple and yet so enjoyable. My guests ask for it over and over again.

1 tablespoon butter
2 tablespoons olive oil
2 cloves garlic, minced
1 large onion, chopped
1 stalk celery with leaves, chopped
3 quarts water
2 pounds chicken wings, tips removed and discarded
1/2 teaspoon fresh thyme
2 large carrots, peeled and cut into 1/2-inch cubes

2 medium white potatoes, peeled and quartered
1/4 pound pumpkin (winter squash), peeled and cubed
1 teaspoon tomato paste
1 quart chicken stock (see recipe on page 52)
1/4 pound vermicelli, broken into small pieces
salt and white pepper to taste
1/4 cup parsley

Heat butter and oil over a moderate flame in a heavy pot and sauté garlic, onion, and celery until onion is tender. Add water, chicken wings, thyme, carrots, potatoes, pumpkin, tomato paste, and chicken stock. Bring to a boil. Reduce heat and simmer covered for 1 hour, or until vegetables are tender. Stir in vermicelli and simmer until vermicelli are soft. Season to taste with salt and pepper. Sprinkle with parsley. *Serves 8.*

Chicken Stock

4 pounds chicken parts (bones, necks, backs, and wings)
3 cloves garlic, peeled and chopped
2 stalks celery with leaves, chopped

2 medium onions, chopped
3 carrots, peeled and chopped
1/2 teaspoon thyme
1/4 cup fresh parsley, chopped
1 bay leaf

Rinse chicken parts. Place chicken parts and all other ingredients in a large stockpot. Pour in enough water to cover. Bring water to a boil. Reduce heat and simmer for 2½ hours. Skim surface of liquid frequently.

Strain stock through a fine sieve or cheesecloth. Cover and refrigerate. *Yields about 3 quarts.*

Mutton Soup

1/4 cup olive oil
1/4 cup butter
2 large onions, chopped
2 stalks celery with leaves,
  chopped
2 cloves garlic, chopped
2 carrots, peeled and chopped
1/4 pound pumpkin (winter
  squash), peeled and chopped
1/2 red pepper, chopped
3 large white potatoes, peeled and
  chopped

2 pounds lamb or mutton, cut
  into 1 1/2-inch cubes
10 cups cold water
1 teaspoon crushed thyme
1/4 teaspoon white pepper
1/2 teaspoon salt
1 bay leaf
1 tablespoon tomato paste
1/4 pound vermicelli, broken into
  small pieces

In a heavy pot, heat oil and butter over a moderate flame. Sauté onions, celery, garlic, carrots, pumpkin, red pepper, potatoes, and lamb for 5 to 7 minutes. Add water, thyme, white pepper, salt, bay leaf, and tomato paste. Cover and simmer for 2 hours, skimming surface occasionally. Stir in vermicelli and simmer uncovered for 10 minutes, or until vermicelli are soft. Correct seasonings. *Serves 8.*

Calf's Foot Soup

1 tablespoon butter
1 tablespoon olive oil
2 large onions, chopped
2 stalks celery with leaves,
   chopped
2 cloves garlic, minced
4 carrots, peeled and chopped
1/2 red pepper, cut into 1-inch
   strips
10 cups cold water
1 calf's foot (approximately 3
   pounds), cut in half lengthwise

1 teaspoon fresh thyme, crushed
1 teaspoon dry mustard
1 teaspoon tomato paste
1/2 teaspoon white pepper
1/2 pound pumpkin (winter
   squash), peeled and chopped
1/2 pound white potatoes, peeled
   and chopped
1/2 pound cabbage, shredded
2 teaspoons salt
1/4 pound shell macaroni

Heat butter and oil in a heavy stockpot. Sauté onions, celery, garlic, carrots, and red pepper for 5 to 7 minutes. Add water, calf's foot, and thyme. Bring water to a boil. Reduce heat and simmer for 1 hour. Skim surface of liquid from time to time. Add mustard, tomato paste, white pepper, pumpkin, potatoes, and cabbage and simmer for another 40 minutes.

In a large pot, bring to boil 2 quarts of water, seasoned with 2 teaspoons of salt. Slowly add macaroni. Boil for about 5 minutes. Drain in colander. Toss to drain well. Add to soup. Simmer for 5 to 10 minutes, or until macaroni is tender. Check seasonings. *Serves 6.*

Lamb or Goat
Head and Foot Soup

2 tablespoons butter
4 tablespoons olive oil
2 large onions, chopped
2 stalks celery with leaves,
   chopped
4 cloves garlic, minced
6 carrots, peeled and chopped
1 lamb or goat foot
   (approximately 3/4 pound), cut
   in half lengthwise
1 lamb or goat head
   (approximately 4 pounds)

8 white potatoes, peeled and
   quartered
12 cups cold water
2 teaspoons crushed thyme
1 bay leaf
1/2 pound pumpkin (winter
   squash), chopped
1 large cabbage, sliced
2 tablespoons tomato paste
1 teaspoon salt
1/2 teaspoon white pepper

Heat butter and oil in a large soup kettle. Add onions, celery, garlic, carrots, foot, head, and potatoes. Cook, stirring occasionally, until head and foot are browned, about 20 minutes. Add water, thyme, and bay leaf. Bring water to a boil. Reduce heat and simmer covered for 1 hour. Skim surface of liquid from time to time.

Remove head and foot pieces. Trim off meat. Discard bones. Cut meat into bite-sized pieces. Return meat to soup kettle. Add pumpkin, cabbage, tomato paste, salt, and pepper. Simmer for 45 minutes. Check seasonings. *Serves 10.*

Breadfruit and Onion Soup

8 cups water
4 cups breadfruit, diced
3 cups onions, chopped
1/2 teaspoon salt
1/4 teaspoon white pepper
6 tablespoons heavy cream

GARNISH
1/2 cup chives, minced

Bring water to a boil in a heavy pot. Add breadfruit, onions, salt, and pepper and simmer for about 45 minutes, or until vegetables are tender. Mash vegetables with a fork or in a blender.

Reheat to a simmer just before serving, add cream, and quickly blend. May be served immediately or chilled and served cold. Garnish with chives in serving dish. *Serves 6.*

Salads

Lobster Salad with Lime Juice

The Caribbean lobster has been called the greatest of culinary delights.

To cook a live lobster: Slowly and carefully lower the lobster into boiling salted water. Boil 15 to 20 minutes. Degree of doneness can be tested by pulling out one of the small legs or swimmerets on the underside of the lobster and examining the meat. After the lobster is done, remove it from the water. Remove the tail section and take out the meat. Split the body and remove meat from each half. A 2-pound lobster yields about ½ pound of meat. Chop into bite-sized pieces. Now you are ready to make the savory salads from Ma Chance's kitchen.

NOTE: For added interest, put a chopped onion, a chopped carrot, and herbs such as thyme, parsley, or tarragon in the boiling liquid 10 minutes before starting to cook the lobster. Sea water may also be used.

1 teaspoon fresh lime juice
2 teaspoons olive oil
1 clove garlic, crushed
salt to taste
freshly ground pepper to taste
1 medium onion, chopped
2 cups cooked lobster meat, diced
  (see cooking directions above)
lettuce leaves

GARNISH
sliced avocado
black olives
hard-boiled eggs
asparagus spears

Mix lime juice with olive oil, garlic, and salt and pepper. Mix well. Toss dressing gently with onion and lobster. Chill for 1 hour. Serve on lettuce leaves, garnish with sliced avocado, black olives, hard-boiled eggs, or asparagus spears. *Serves 4.*

Lobster Salad #2

2 cups cooked lobster meat, diced
(see cooking directions on
p. 59)
1 tablespoon onion, grated
2 tablespoons celery with leaves,
chopped
2 tablespoons green pepper,
chopped
1/2 cup mayonnaise
1 teaspoon fresh lime juice

1/2 teaspoon salt
dash of cayenne sauce, or 5 drops
Tabasco
1 tablespoon dry mustard
lettuce leaves

GARNISH
paprika
black olives
sliced avocado

In a salad bowl, combine lobster, onion, celery, and green pepper. In a mixing bowl, combine mayonnaise, lime juice, salt, cayenne or Tabasco, and mustard. Mix well. Toss dressing gently over lobster and vegetables. Cover and chill for 1 hour. Serve on bed of lettuce leaves and garnish with paprika, black olives, and sliced avocado. Serves 4.

Codfish and Vegetable Salad

1/2 pound salt codfish
1 tablespoon lemon juice
1 cup cooked green peas
1 tablespoon sweet pickle,
   chopped
1/2 cup cooked carrots, chopped
1 medium sweet potato, cooked
   and cut into bite-sized pieces
2 tablespoons mayonnaise

1 tablespoon olive oil
3 drops Tabasco
salt to taste
pepper to taste
lettuce leaves

GARNISH
1 to 2 tomatoes, sliced
1 avocado, sliced

To remove salt, soak codfish in cold water for 12 hours. Drain. Place in boiling water to cover and simmer 3 to 4 minutes. Drain. Remove bones and cut into 3/4-inch cubes.

Combine all ingredients *except* salt and pepper and mix well. Season with salt and pepper. Chill. Serve on lettuce leaves and garnish with sliced tomato and avocado. *Serves 2 to 4.*

Whelk Salad

Whelks are very much like escargots, except that escargots are land snails and whelks (periwinkles) are sea snails. They cling to the reefs in the sea and are pulled off by hand. Their taste is similar to that of escargots but stronger.

To shell whelks: Boil whelks in their shells. A bushel of baby whelks in the shell (about 200) yields about 2 pounds of meat. Shelling them is a pleasant, sociable activity for two or three people to do together. They are very tasty, so you have to be careful not to eat too many while you're shelling them!

Whelks come out of their shells very easily. Simply remove the cap on top before pulling the whelk from the shell with a large pin. After taking the whelks out of their shells, clean them under cold running water.

1 cup water
2 pounds shelled whelks (see shelling directions above)
2 cloves garlic, crushed
1 tablespoon lime juice
2 tablespoons olive oil
1/4 teaspoon Tabasco

pinch of salt and pepper
lettuce leaves

GARNISH
1 medium onion, sliced
1 green pepper, sliced

In a saucepan, bring water to a boil and add whelks, garlic, lime juice, olive oil, Tabasco, salt, and pepper. Simmer for 20 to 30 minutes. Drain and cool. Serve on a bed of lettuce leaves, garnish with onion and green pepper. *Serves 6.*

Chicken Salad

2 whole chicken breasts
2 cups chicken broth
1 onion, whole
1 carrot, sliced
pinch of thyme
1/2 bay leaf
1 sweet red pepper
1 ripe avocado

1 tablespoon fresh tarragon,
    chopped
1 tablespoon fresh chives, chopped
1 tablespoon red wine vinegar
salt and pepper to taste
2 tablespoons olive oil
2 tablespoons corn oil
lettuce leaves

Poach chicken breasts in chicken broth simmered with onion, carrot, thyme, and bay leaf for about 20 minutes. Remove chicken from poaching liquid and allow to cool at room temperature.

Seed and devein red pepper and slice into thin strips (almost slivers). Peel and halve avocado, remove pit, and slice thinly.

When chicken is cool enough to handle, remove meat from bone in one piece. Slice boned breasts crosswise into 1/4-inch slices. Toss chicken pieces, red pepper slices, and avocado slices together with chopped fresh herbs. In a small bowl, mix red wine vinegar with pinch of salt and pepper. Mix in olive oil and corn oil. Pour into bowl with chicken and vegetables and toss to mix. Refrigerate until ready to use. Serve on lettuce leaves. *Serves 4.*

Salt Codfish Salad

1/2 pound boneless salt codfish, flaked
2 tablespoons olive oil
1 teaspoon white wine vinegar
1 large onion, minced
1 clove garlic, crushed

1 large red pepper, chopped
lettuce leaves

GARNISH
1 to 2 tomatoes, sliced
black olives

To remove salt, soak codfish in cold water for 12 hours. Drain. Boil in water to cover for 3 to 4 minutes. Drain. Set aside in a salad bowl.

In a mixing bowl, combine olive oil, vinegar, onion, garlic, and red pepper. Blend thoroughly. Pour dressing over codfish and toss lightly. Chill for 1 hour. Serve on a bed of lettuce leaves; garnish with sliced tomatoes and black olives. *Serves 2 to 4.*

Tuna and Macaroni Salad

8 ounces small shell macaroni
1 cup mayonnaise
juice of 1/2 lime
7 ounces tuna, drained and flaked
1/4 cup onion, finely chopped
1/4 cup celery with leaves, finely
  chopped
1 teaspoon fresh thyme
1/4 cup green pepper, finely
  chopped

1/4 teaspoon salt
freshly ground black pepper
  to taste
lettuce leaves

GARNISH
8 cooked asparagus tips
2 tomatoes, sliced
1 avocado, sliced

Cook macaroni in 2 quarts of boiling water. Add 1 teaspoon salt, if desired. Boil rapidly, stirring occasionally, for 10 to 12 minutes. Drain. Rinse with cold water.

In a mixing bowl, combine mayonnaise and lime juice. Add macaroni and blend well.

In a separate bowl, combine tuna, onion, celery, thyme, green pepper, salt, and black pepper. Add to macaroni mixture. Toss gently. Chill for at least 2 hours. Stir occasionally. Serve on a bed of lettuce leaves; garnish with cooked asparagus tips, tomatoes, and sliced avocado. *Serves 4.*

Cole Slaw

1/2 pound white or red cabbage,
  shredded
1 or 2 large carrots, shredded
1/2 cup cooked green peas
lettuce leaves

DRESSING
1/2 cup mayonnaise
1 teaspoon dry mustard
2 tablespoons tarragon vinegar
1 tablespoon lime juice

1 clove garlic, crushed
1 teaspoon sugar
2 tablespoons onion, minced
1 red pepper, chopped
1/4 teaspoon freshly ground white
  pepper
1/2 teaspoon salt

GARNISH
fresh pineapple chunks

In a salad bowl, toss cabbage, carrots, and peas. Set aside. In a mixing
bowl, combine mayonnaise, mustard, vinegar, lime juice, garlic, sugar,
onion, red pepper, white pepper, and salt. Mix thoroughly. Pour
dressing over slaw. Blend well. Chill for 2 hours. Serve on a bed of
lettuce leaves; garnish with fresh pineapple chunks. *Serves 2 to 4.*

Fresh Fruit Salad

1 cup papaya, diced
1 cup banana, sliced
1 cup pineapple, cubed
1 cup orange, in sections
1 cup grapefruit, in sections
1 cup mango, diced

juice of 1 lime
1/8 cup rum

GARNISH
fresh mint, chopped

In mixing bowl, blend all ingredients and chill. Serve garnished with
chopped fresh mint. *Serves 8.*

Breadfruit Salad

1 medium breadfruit
1 teaspoon salt
1 cup cooked green peas
lettuce leaves

DRESSING
1 teaspoon dry mustard
1 teaspoon salt
1/4 teaspoon thyme
1/4 teaspoon freshly ground
   black pepper
1/4 teaspoon paprika

1/2 teaspoon sugar
3 tablespoons mayonnaise
1 clove garlic, crushed
1 small onion, grated
1/4 cup tarragon vinegar
1/4 cup olive oil
1/2 cup vegetable oil

GARNISH
fresh parsley
3 to 4 tomatoes, sliced

Peel, core, and cut breadfruit into 1-inch cubes. Place breadfruit in saucepan with salted water to cover and bring to a boil over medium heat. Boil for 15 to 20 minutes, or until tender when pricked with a fork. Drain and cool. Place breadfruit in a mixing bowl.

In a separate bowl, combine mustard, salt, thyme, black pepper, paprika, sugar, mayonnaise, garlic, onion, vinegar, olive oil, and vegetable oil. Mix well. Add peas to breadfruit. Pour dressing over breadfruit and toss to mix well. Chill for at least 2 hours. Serve on lettuce leaves and garnish with fresh parsley and sliced tomatoes. *Serves 6 to 8.*

Tossed Green Salad

1/2 clove garlic
1 pound Boston, Bibb, or leaf
  lettuce
1 medium tomato, cut into
  thin wedges
1 cucumber, thinly sliced
1 small green pepper, seeded,
  deveined, and chopped
1 small sweet red pepper, seeded,
  deveined, and chopped

VINAIGRETTE
1 tablespoon red wine vinegar
1 tablespoon olive oil
2 tablespoons corn oil
1/2 teaspoon dry mustard
1/2 teaspoon fresh thyme, minced
salt and pepper to taste

Wipe inside of a salad bowl with garlic. Wash lettuce and pat dry. Break lettuce into pieces and place in salad bowl. Add tomato, cucumber, green pepper, and red pepper. Mix and refrigerate to keep crisp.

In a small mixing bowl, combine vinegar, olive oil, corn oil, mustard, thyme, and salt and pepper to taste. Blend thoroughly with a wire whisk or egg beater. Pour over salad just before serving and toss thoroughly. *Serves 6.*

Fish
and
Seafood

Fish and seafood have always been among the most important ingredients in the foods of St. Martin. The freshness of our seafood adds a special savor. Our local fishermen leave for the sea in their boats as the sun is coming up and return in late afternoon. The size of the catch depends on their luck.

I always have fresh seafood on my menu. When I serve red snapper, kingfish, yellowtail, conch, or lobster, it usually has been caught that day.

Stuffed Baked Fish

Many different types of fish may be used for this recipe. I am especially fond of red snapper, yellowtail, or a small kingfish.

*1 4-pound fish, cut for stuffing
  and boned*
salt to taste
1/4 teaspoon pepper
2 slices bacon
4 tablespoons olive oil
2 medium onions, chopped
1 medium green pepper, chopped
1 stalk celery, chopped
2 cloves garlic, crushed

1 tomato, chopped
1/4 teaspoon Tabasco (optional)
1 cup breadcrumbs
4 tablespoons butter, melted
1 lemon, sliced

GARNISH
3 slices lemon or lime
fresh parsley

Preheat oven to 325°.

Rinse fish and drain on paper towel. Season with salt and pepper and let stand.

In a skillet, cook bacon until crisp. Remove bacon and drain on paper towel. Discard grease. In the same skillet, heat olive oil over a moderate flame and add onions, green pepper, celery, garlic, tomato, and Tabasco. Stir and cover. Simmer for 5 minutes. Add breadcrumbs and crumbled bacon. Blend well. Simmer for 3 minutes.

Stuff fish with mixture. Stitch with heavy thread. Baste fish with melted butter. Place lemon slices down center of fish. Wrap fish in aluminum foil and place in a baking dish. Bake 40 to 45 minutes. Remove foil and brown on each side until fish is golden brown, 8 to 10 minutes. Place on serving platter and pour on pan juice in desired amount. Garnish with lemon or lime and fresh parsley. *Serves 8.*

Fish and Vegetable Casserole

I prefer red snapper or yellowtail for this casserole, but any firm fish, such as halibut, haddock, or salmon, will do.

2 pounds fish
1 large carrot, cubed
2 medium white potatoes, peeled
   and cubed
1/2 pound pumpkin (winter
   squash), peeled and cubed
1 large onion, chopped
1 cup white rice, cooked

1/4 teaspoon Tabasco (optional)
2 cloves garlic, crushed
1/4 teaspoon crushed thyme
salt to taste
freshly ground pepper to taste
1 tablespoon olive oil
2 tablespoons breadcrumbs
2 tablespoons butter

Preheat oven to 350°.

Poach fish in court bouillon (see recipe on page 88) for 5 to 10 minutes. Remove bones and skin. Set aside. In a separate pot, bring vegetables to boil for about 15 minutes. Drain. In a bowl, mix together fish, vegetables, rice, Tabasco, and seasonings. Place in a casserole lightly greased with olive oil. Cover with breadcrumbs. Dot top with butter. Bake for about 15 minutes, or until casserole is bubbling and breadcrumbs are brown. *Serves 6.*

Poached Kingfish

2 pounds fish, with bones and
   head, slit lengthwise and
   gutted
1 lime, quartered
1 teaspoon salt
2 cloves garlic, crushed
1/4 teaspoon black pepper
1 tablespoon white wine vinegar
2 tablespoons butter
2 tablespoons olive oil

1 stalk celery, chopped
1 onion, sliced in rounds
1 red pepper, sliced in rounds
1 tomato, peeled, seeded, and
   sliced
1 teaspoon dry mustard
1 tablespoon tomato paste
2 cups water
1/4 teaspoon cayenne pepper
1 teaspoon lime juice

Rinse and dry fish. Rub inside with lime. Mix salt, garlic, pepper, and vinegar and put inside fish. Marinate for 30 minutes.

In a large skillet, heat butter and olive oil over a moderate flame and sauté celery, onion, and red pepper until onion is translucent. Add tomato, mustard, and tomato paste and simmer and stir for about 3 minutes. Add water, bring to a boil, and carefully lower fish into boiling liquid. Adjust heat so that liquid is slowly simmering. Cover tightly and simmer for 15 to 20 minutes, or until tender.

Remove fish to a hot platter and keep warm. Add cayenne to liquid, check seasonings. If flavor seems weak, raise heat and boil to reduce liquid slightly. Add lime juice and serve with hot corn balls (see recipe on page 75) and pigeon peas and rice (see recipe on p. 108). *Serves 6.*

Red Snapper Fillets

1/2 pound red snapper fillets
juice of 1/2 lime
1/2 cup butter, melted
freshly ground pepper to taste

paprika to taste
salt to taste
2 tablespoons fresh parsley,
  chopped

Rinse and dry fish. Place in a shallow baking pan. Cover with lime juice. Brush with butter and sprinkle with seasonings. Broil until brown, about 5 to 8 minutes. Turn, brush with butter, and sprinkle with seasonings again. Broil until fish is brown and flakes easily with a fork, about 5 minutes again. Be careful not to overcook. Garnish with fresh chopped parsley and serve at once. *Serves 2.*

Baked Lobster

2 tablespoons melted butter
1 tablespoon lime juice
3 drops Tabasco
2 cloves garlic, minced

1/4 cup celery, minced
freshly ground pepper to taste
1 medium lobster, about 2 1/2
  pounds

Preheat oven to 450°.

Mix butter, lime juice, and all other ingredients *except* lobster. Cut lobster in half lengthwise and place cut side up in a shallow baking pan. Baste with butter mixture. Bake until done, about 20 minutes. Baste twice during baking. *Serves 2.*

Lobster Stew
with Hot Corn Balls

1 1/2 pounds lobster meat, cut
    into bite-sized pieces
3 tablespoons butter
3 tablespoons olive oil
1 large onion, sliced
2 cloves garlic, crushed
1/4 green pepper, sliced
1 stalk celery with leaves,
    chopped

4 cups hot water
1/4 teaspoon crushed thyme
1 tablespoon vinegar
1/4 teaspoon freshly ground pepper
salt to taste
1 tomato, sliced
hot cornballs (see recipe below)

In a heavy skillet, sauté lobster meat in butter and olive oil with onion, garlic, green pepper, and celery until onion is tender. Add water and bring to a boil. Add all remaining ingredients *except* tomato. Simmer for 30 minutes. Add sliced tomato on top and simmer for another 3 to 4 minutes. Serve with hot corn balls. *Serves 4.*

HOT CORN BALLS

2 1/4 cups water
1/2 teaspoon salt
1 cup yellow cornmeal
1 tablespoon sugar

2 tablespoons butter
2 egg yolks, beaten
2 egg whites

Preheat oven to 425°.

In a saucepan, combine water and salt. Bring to a boil. Stir in cornmeal gradually. Add sugar and butter. Mix thoroughly. Simmer about 10 minutes until mixture thickens. Remove from heat and let cool. Add beaten egg yolks. Blend well. Beat egg whites until stiff. Fold in egg whites. Blend well.

Form balls with tablespoons of batter. Set in a lightly greased 2-inch high jelly roll pan. Bake for 20 minutes. *Makes 10 to 12 balls.*

Crab Burgers

To prepare the crabs: In a large pot, place 1 whole onion and 1 carrot. Add 2 to 3 quarts of salted water and bring to a boil. Add live crabs and boil for 20 minutes. The shells will change color when properly cooked. Remove crabs from pot and cool. Remove meat from shells and rinse in warm water. Remove cartilage from meat.

*2 cups crabmeat, or 14 to 16
    crabs
2 tablespoons butter, melted
1 green pepper, minced
1 stalk celery, minced
1 medium onion, minced
1 cup mayonnaise
salt to taste*

*4 drops Worcestershire sauce
dash of Tabasco or cayenne
    pepper
lemon juice to taste
freshly ground pepper to taste
8 slices French bread, or
    8 johnnycakes
1 cup cheddar cheese, grated*

Prepare crabs according to the directions above. In a skillet, heat butter and sauté green pepper, celery, and onion until vegetables are tender. In a bowl, mix crabmeat, mayonnaise, and sautéed vegetables. Add salt, Worcestershire sauce, Tabasco, lemon juice, and pepper. Blend well.

Place French bread on a cookie sheet. Baste bread with melted butter from skillet. Brown lightly in broiler. Remove from oven and spread crabmeat mixture on bread slices. Sprinkle with cheese. Broil about 4 inches from heat until cheese is melted. Serve at once. *Serves 8.*

Stewed Codfish
with Eggs and Tomatoes

1 *pound salt codfish*
2 *tablespoons butter*
1 *tablespoon olive oil*
1 *medium onion, sliced*
1 *tablespoon white wine vinegar*
1/2 cup water

GARNISH
2 *tomatoes, sliced*
4 *hard-boiled eggs, sliced*
1/2 red pepper, sliced

To remove salt, soak codfish in cold water for 12 hours. Drain. Place in boiling water to cover and simmer for 5 minutes. Remove bones and cut into ¾-inch cubes.

In a heavy skillet, heat butter and olive oil over moderate flame and sauté onion until tender. Add codfish, vinegar, and water and simmer for 30 minutes.

Place codfish on platter and add sauce from skillet. Garnish with slices of tomato, egg, and red pepper. *Serves 2.*

Codfish and Eggplant

1 1/2 pounds salt codfish
2 medium onions, sliced
1/4 red pepper, sliced
1 stalk celery, chopped
1/4 teaspoon black pepper
2 tablespoons butter

4 tablespoons olive oil
4 to 5 medium eggplants, peeled
    and seeded, cut into slices
    about 3/4-inch thick
1 teaspoon white wine vinegar
1 tomato, sliced

To remove salt, soak codfish in cold water for 12 hours. Drain. Boil in water to cover for 3 to 4 minutes. Drain. Remove bones and cut into 1-inch cubes.

In a heavy skillet, sauté onions, red pepper, celery, and black pepper in butter and olive oil until vegetables are tender, about 10 minutes. Remove with a slotted spoon and set aside.

In the same skillet, fry eggplant over low heat until golden brown, about 5 minutes on each side. Add codfish, sautéed vegetables, vinegar, and tomato and simmer for about 6 minutes. *Serves 6.*

Codfish and Curry Rice

1 pound salt codfish
1 large onion, chopped
1 green pepper, chopped
1 tablespoon olive oil

3 drops Tabasco
1 cup rice
1/2 teaspoon curry powder
3 cups water

To remove salt, soak codfish in cold water for 12 hours. Drain. Place in boiling water to cover and simmer for 3 to 4 minutes. Drain. Remove bones and cut into 3/4-inch cubes.

In a heavy skillet, sauté onion and green pepper in olive oil until tender. Remove vegetables with a slotted spoon and pour off oil. In a heavy pot, combine fish, vegetables, Tabasco, rice, curry powder, and water. Cover and simmer until rice is done, about 20 minutes. *Serves 6.*

Codfish and Dumplings

1 pound codfish
dumplings (see recipe on page 45)
1 large onion, chopped
2 tablespoons butter

1 tablespoon olive oil
1/4 teaspoon thyme
1 1/2 cups water
1 tablespoon white wine vinegar

To remove salt, soak codfish in cold water for 12 hours. Drain. Boil in water to cover for 3 to 4 minutes. Drain. Remove bones and cut into 3/4-inch pieces.

Prepare dumplings.

In a heavy pot, sauté onion in butter and olive oil until onion is tender. Add codfish, thyme, water, and vinegar. Simmer for 10 minutes. Add dumplings and simmer covered for another 15 minutes. *Serves 6.*

Fried Codfish

1 pound salt codfish
corn oil for deep frying
2 medium onions, sliced

2 tablespoons butter
3 drops Tabasco
1 teaspoon white wine vinegar

To remove salt, soak codfish in water for 12 hours. Drain. Boil in water to cover for 3 to 4 minutes. Place in very cold water for 5 minutes to help solidify the flesh. Pat dry with paper towel and cut into bite-sized pieces. In a separate pan, deep fry codfish until it becomes golden, about 10 minutes. Place on paper towel to remove excess oil.

In a heavy skillet, sauté onions in butter until golden. Mix together sautéed onions, Tabasco, and vinegar. Place fish on platter and sprinkle onion mixture on top. *Serves 2.*

Steamed Cherrystone Clams

4 dozen cherrystone clams
salt to taste
freshly ground pepper to taste
3 drops Tabasco or cayenne
  pepper

1 cup water
1 teaspoon fresh lime juice
1/2 cup butter, melted

Scrub clams under cold running water with a stiff brush. Wash in several waters. Place clams close together in the top of a steamer and sprinkle with salt, pepper, and Tabasco. Place water in bottom of the steamer. Cover pot and steam clams over moderate heat until shells open, no longer than 5 to 10 minutes. Remove clams. Strain clam broth through cheesecloth and reserve about 1/2 cup.

Serve clams hot in shells. Add lime juice to reserved liquid. To eat, remove clams from shells and dip in a bowl of broth and a bowl of melted butter. *Serves 6 to 8.*

Fried Clams

4 cups pancake mix (see recipe
  on page 30)

1 quart clams, drained
corn oil for frying

In a mixing bowl, prepare pancake mix. Add clams, a few at a time, until well coated. Shake off excess pancake mix, using a wire basket. Deep fry (375°) until golden brown, about 4 to 5 minutes. Drain on paper towel. Serve hot with Ma Chance's Hot Pepper Sauce (see recipe on p. 40). *Serves 8.*

Conch and Papaya

2 pounds conch meat
juice of 2 limes
1 1/2 quarts water

2 half-ripe papayas
fresh mint

Prepare conch meat according to the method on p. 50. Cut into strips and put in a pressure cooker with boiling water. Cook for 20 minutes. Remove pressure cooker from heat or place pot under cold running water to reduce pressure. When hissing stops, remove pressure gauge. Top can now be removed.

Add papayas and simmer covered (without pressure gauge) until tender, about 30 minutes. Serve with fresh mint. *Serves 10.*

Conch Stew

2 pounds conch meat
juice of 2 limes
3 tablespoons butter
1 tablespoon olive oil
1 large onion, chopped
1 green pepper, chopped
2 large tomatoes, peeled and
    sliced

1 1/2 cups chicken broth
1/2 teaspoon curry powder
    (optional)
dash of Tabasco, or minced hot
    pepper
1 1/2 tablespoons fresh parsley,
    chopped

Prepare conch meat according to the method on page 50. Cut into bite-sized pieces.

In an uncovered pressure cooker, heat butter and olive oil and sauté conch, onion, and green pepper until vegetables are tender. Add remaining ingredients. Cook under pressure for 20 minutes. Serve at once in large soup bowls and sprinkle with parsley. *Serves 6.*

Conch and Macaroni

4 pounds conch meat
juice of 4 limes
1 pound small pasta shells
3 tablespoons butter
2 tablespoons olive oil

1 cup milk
salt and pepper to taste
4 tablespoons cheddar cheese,
  grated

Preheat oven to 350°.

Prepare conch meat according to the method on page 50. Cook pasta in boiling water for 5 minutes. Drain thoroughly and set aside. Mince conch in food processor or meat grinder. In a heavy saucepan, heat butter and olive oil over a moderate flame. Add pasta and conch and simmer for 5 minutes. Add milk, salt, and pepper. Mix well. Place mixture in a baking dish and sprinkle cheese on top. Bake until golden brown, about 15 minutes. *Serves 10.*

Conch and Curry Rice

3 pounds conch meat, cut into
  bite-sized pieces
juice of 3 limes
1 medium onion, sliced
1/2 green pepper, chopped
1 stalk celery, chopped
3 tablespoons butter
1 teaspoon olive oil

1 tablespoon tomato paste
1/2 teaspoon salt
1/2 teaspoon cayenne pepper
1 1/2 quarts water
1 1/2 cups rice
4 slices uncooked ham, chopped
1/2 teaspoon curry powder

Prepare conch according to the method on page 50. In an uncovered
pressure cooker, sauté onion, green pepper, and celery in butter and
olive oil, until onion is tender. Add conch, tomato paste, salt, cayenne, and water. Cover pressure cooker and cook for 20 minutes.

    Remove pressure cooker from heat and let pressure drop, or put
pot under cold running water. When pressure drops, remove top.
Add rice, ham, and curry powder and stir. Cover (without pressure
gauge) and simmer until rice is cooked, about 30 minutes. *Serves 10.*

Deviled Crab Deluxe

16 medium crabs, or 2 cups
  crabmeat
2 onions, one whole and
  one minced
1 carrot
2 cups breadcrumbs
4 tablespoons butter, melted
1/4 cup fresh parsley, chopped

1 teaspoon dry mustard
2 dashes of Tabasco
Worcestershire sauce to taste
1 tablespoon lemon juice
salt to taste
pepper to taste
1/4 cup evaporated milk
melted butter to dab on top

Preheat oven to 350°.

Prepare crabs according to the method on page 76. Retain shells.

In a bowl, mix crabmeat, 1/2 cup of breadcrumbs, 4 tablespoons of butter, and all remaining ingredients *except* extra breadcrumbs and melted butter for top. Blend lightly but thoroughly. Put mixture into crab shells, sprinkle with remaining breadcrumbs, dot with melted butter. Bake in oven for 12 to 15 minutes, or until brown on top. *Serves 8.*

Crabmeat Royale

16 medium crabs
2 onions, one whole and
  one minced
1 carrot
1/4 pound fresh mushrooms,
  cleaned and thinly sliced
1/4 cup butter

Worcestershire sauce to taste
2 tablespoons flour
1 cup milk
salt to taste
pepper to taste
2 tablespoons cheddar cheese,
  grated

Preheat oven to 350°.

Prepare crabs according to the method on page 76. Retain shells.

In a large skillet, sauté mushrooms and minced onion in butter until onion is tender. Add crabmeat and Worcestershire sauce and blend.

In a bowl, mix flour and milk until smooth and creamy. Add to crabmeat mixture. Stir constantly for 5 minutes over moderate heat until mixture is well blended. Add salt and pepper and blend.

Fill crab shells with mixture. Sprinkle grated cheese on top. Bake in oven until cheese melts, about 5 minutes. *Serves 8.*

Turtle Steak

2 pounds turtle steak, boneless
4 cloves garlic, crushed
1/2 teaspoon salt
4 cloves, crushed
1/4 teaspoon ground black pepper
1/2 cup vinegar
3/4 cup white wine
1/2 teaspoon crushed thyme
1/4 teaspoon Tabasco, or 3 dashes
  of cayenne

1 teaspoon olive oil
1 tablespoon butter
1 large onion, sliced
1 stalk celery, chopped
1/2 red pepper, sliced
1/2 cup water
1 tablespoon tomato paste
1 tomato, chopped

With a sharp knife, make slits about 1/4 inch deep all over the turtle steak. Mix garlic, salt, cloves, and black pepper and stuff in slits. Place steak in a bowl. Combine vinegar, 1/2 cup of the wine, thyme, and Tabasco. Pour over steak and marinate for 1 to 2 hours.

Pour off liquid from turtle steak and reserve. In a heavy pot, heat olive oil and butter over moderate flame. Sauté meat in oil until brown, about 20 minutes. Add reserved liquid. Cover and simmer for 30 minutes. Add onion, celery, red pepper, water, and remaining 1/4 cup of white wine. Simmer for another 30 minutes.

Add tomato paste and tomato and simmer for 10 minutes. Remove steak from pot and place on platter. Slice steak and cover with sauce from pot. *Serves 8.*

Turtle Stew

2 pounds turtle stew meat
  (mixture of bones and meat)
2 tablespoons olive oil
2 tablespoons butter
2 cloves garlic, crushed
2 large onions, sliced
1 stalk celery, chopped
1/4 green pepper, chopped
1/2 teaspoon crushed thyme

1/2 teaspoon parsley
3 cloves
1/4 teaspoon Tabasco
1 bay leaf
1/2 teaspoon oregano
1 tomato, sliced
1 teaspoon salt
pepper to taste
1/2 cup dry white wine

Place bones in boiling water to cover and let stand for about 5 minutes, until the shell-like skin can be removed from the bones. Remove and discard skin. Boil bones until they become jellylike, about 10 or 15 minutes.

In a large heavy pot, place meat and bones in fresh boiling water to cover. Simmer for 1 hour.

Heat oil and butter in a skillet over a moderate flame and sauté garlic, onions, celery, and green pepper until onions are tender. With a slotted spoon, remove vegetables and add to pot. Add all remaining ingredients *except* wine and simmer covered until meat is tender, 1 hour. Add wine and simmer for 10 more minutes. *Serves 6.*

Court Bouillon

2 medium carrots, thinly sliced
1 medium onion, thinly sliced
5 shallots, chopped
1 stalk celery
2 cloves garlic, unpeeled and
  chopped
1 bay leaf
1/4 teaspoon thyme

1 tablespoon fresh parsley,
  chopped
1 lime with rind, quartered
  and squeezed
salt to taste
2 cups dry white wine
1 1/2 quarts water

Combine all ingredients in a large kettle. Bring to a boil, reduce heat, and simmer for 30 minutes. Skim occasionally. Strain liquid. Refrigerate or freeze until ready to use in poaching seafood. *Yields 1 1/2 quarts.*

Poultry

Ma Chance's
Chicken and Shrimp Creole

2 tablespoons olive oil
2 tablespoons butter
1/2 pound baby shrimp,
  unshelled
2 cups chicken broth
1 3- to 4-pound chicken, cut into
  serving pieces
1 onion, chopped

1 sweet red pepper, seeded
  and sliced
2 cloves garlic, chopped
1 cup rice
1 tablespoon saffron threads,
  crushed
salt and pepper to taste

In a large skillet, heat olive oil and butter over a moderate flame. Quickly sauté shrimp until they begin to turn red, 1 to 2 minutes. Remove from skillet and set aside. Set skillet aside. Remove shells from shrimp. Reserve shells.

In a separate heavy pot, simmer chicken broth with shrimp shells. In the skillet, brown chicken pieces on all sides until golden. Remove and set aside. Lower heat to medium low and sauté onion, red pepper, and garlic until onion is tender. Add rice and saffron and stir constantly until rice is thoroughly coated with oil.

Return shrimp to skillet and stir. Strain simmered broth into skillet and place chicken pieces on top. Cover and simmer until all liquid is absorbed, about 30 minutes. Season with salt and pepper. Garnish with lime wedges. *Serves 4.*

Marinated Grilled Chicken

1/4 cup olive oil
1/2 cup dry white wine
juice of 2 limes
1 clove garlic, minced
1 small onion, thickly sliced

salt and pepper to taste
1/4 teaspoon dried thyme
1 3-pound chicken, cut into
   serving pieces
additional olive oil for basting

Mix olive oil, wine, lime juice, garlic, onion, thyme, and pinch of salt and pepper in a bowl large enough to hold chicken pieces. Toss to coat all pieces of chicken with marinade and onion slices. Marinate for 2 hours in the refrigerator. Stir several times while marinating.

Remove chicken from marinade and dry on paper towel. Remove any onion slices that cling and return them to marinade liquid.

Either broil chicken or grill it over glowing coals until pieces are done. Begin with legs, after 10 to 15 minutes add breasts and wings, continue to broil or grill until done. Frequently brush the cooking pieces with olive oil and marinade liquid. Serve with Ma Chance's Hot Pepper Sauce (see recipe on p. 40). *Serves 4.*

Chicken and Papaya

1 *lime*
salt and pepper to taste
1 *3-pound chicken, cut into*
  serving pieces
2 *tablespoons butter*
1 *tablespoon corn oil*

1 *cup chicken broth*
pinch of thyme
1 *firm papaya, peeled, seeded,*
  and diced
1 *tablespoon fresh mint, chopped*

Squeeze lime and mix juice with pinch of salt and pepper in a large bowl. Toss cut-up chicken with juice and leave to marinate at room temperature for 15 to 20 minutes. Toss frequently.

In a heavy skillet, heat butter and oil over medium flame. Dry chicken pieces on paper towel. Add to hot butter and oil and sauté to brown on both sides, about 7 to 10 minutes. Add chicken broth and pinch of thyme. Stir and bring to a boil. Cover and simmer for 10 minutes. Add papaya pieces, cover, and simmer for 7 to 10 minutes. Garnish with fresh mint. *Serves 4.*

Chicken and Dumplings

1 4-pound chicken, trussed
1 pound chicken necks and
  gizzards
2 cloves garlic, chopped
2 stalks celery with leaves,
  chopped
1 medium onion, sliced
1/2 teaspoon thyme
4 large carrots, peeled and
  chopped
1/4 cup fresh parsley, chopped

1 hot red pepper, seeded and
  chopped
1 teaspoon salt (or to taste)
1/4 teaspoon freshly ground pepper
1/4 pound pumpkin (winter
  squash), peeled, seeded, and
  cubed
2 cups string beans, cut into
  1-inch pieces
dumplings (see recipe on p. 45)

In a large stockpot, combine chicken, chicken parts, garlic, celery, onion, thyme, carrots, parsley, red pepper, salt, and pepper. Add cold water to cover. Bring to a boil. Reduce heat, cover, and simmer for 60 minutes, skimming surface frequently. Add pumpkin and string beans. Simmer for 30 minutes, or until chicken and vegetables are tender. Add dumplings. Cover tightly and simmer for 12 to 15 minutes. Remove chicken and carve. Serve with dumplings and vegetables. *Serves 6.*

Chicken and Mango

2 whole chicken breasts, split,
  skinned, and boned
1/2 teaspoon salt
1/2 teaspoon white pepper
1/2 teaspoon freshly ground
  nutmeg

2 tablespoons butter
1 onion, thinly sliced
2 tablespoons chutney
1/2 cup white wine
1 ripe mango, sliced
1/4 cup heavy cream

Rinse chicken and pat dry. In a small bowl, mix salt, pepper, and nutmeg. Dredge chicken in seasonings. In a large skillet, heat butter over a moderate flame and sauté onion until tender. Add chicken and sauté lightly on both sides. Spread chutney on chicken. Add wine to skillet. Cover and simmer for 10 minutes.

Remove chicken to serving dish. Garnish with mango. Add heavy cream to liquid in skillet. Stir and simmer until sauce thickens, about 3 to 5 minutes. Pour sauce over chicken and mango slices. *Serves 4.*

Meat

Beef and Dumplings

2 pounds stew beef, cubed
2 tablespoons red wine vinegar
salt to taste
2 cloves garlic, crushed
1/2 teaspoon pepper
1/4 cup corn oil
1 large onion, sliced
1 medium red pepper, sliced

1 teaspoon tomato paste
Tabasco to taste
1/2 teaspoon thyme
1/2 bay leaf
1 1/2 tablespoons parsley, chopped
2 cups water
dumplings (see recipe on p. 45)

Rinse meat. In a bowl, combine vinegar, salt, garlic, and pepper. Add meat. Marinate for 30 minutes at room temperature, stirring frequently. Discard marinade.

In a large skillet, brown meat on all sides in hot oil. When meat is browned, lower heat and add sliced onion, pepper, tomato paste, Tabasco, thyme, bay leaf, and parsley. Cover and simmer slowly for 5 minutes. Add water, stir thoroughly. Cover and simmer until meat is tender when a fork is inserted, about 1½ hours.

When meat is tender, add dumplings and simmer covered for 12 to 15 minutes. It may be necessary to add more liquid before adding the dumplings. *Serves 2 to 4.*

Roast Leg of Lamb or Goat

Legs of goat and lamb taste very different. But each can be roasted or pot-roasted. Here is the way I do it.

10-pound leg of lamb or goat
1/2 teaspoon salt
1 teaspoon freshly ground pepper
4 cloves garlic, minced

1 small onion, minced
2 to 3 drops Worcestershire sauce
sprigs of fresh parsley

Preheat oven to 350°.

Make a slit about 6½ inches long and ½ inch deep on each side of the meat. Mix together salt, pepper, garlic, onion, and Worcestershire sauce. Rub into slits. Let stand for 30 to 45 minutes.

Wrap meat in aluminum foil. Place in a roasting pan, fat side up, and bake for 5 hours (30 to 35 minutes per pound). Garnish with parsley. *Serves 8.*

Pot-Roasted Leg of Lamb, Pork, or Goat

4-pound leg of pork (fresh ham),
    lamb, or goat
1/4 cup corn oil
1/2 cup water
1/2 teaspoon salt
2 cloves garlic, minced
1/2 teaspoon pepper

1 small onion, chopped
2 to 3 drops Worcestershire sauce
1/2 teaspoon thyme
1 teaspoon fresh parsley, chopped
1 bay leaf
1 medium carrot, chopped
1 tomato, chopped

In a heavy pot, brown meat on all sides in corn oil over medium heat. Add water and all remaining ingredients *except* tomato. Cover tightly and simmer gently until meat is tender, about 3 hours. Add water if needed. Add tomato 15 minutes before meat is done. *Serves 4.*

Pickled Pigs' Ears
and Vegetables

1 pound pigs' ears
salt to taste
6 green plantains, peeled and cut
  in half crosswise
2 sweet potatoes, peeled and cut
  in half

2 tablespoons white wine vinegar
1 clove garlic, crushed
1 teaspoon allspice
2 medium onions, chopped
1 hot pepper, chopped
3 cloves

Scrub pigs' ears thoroughly in hot water until they are white. In a heavy pot, place meat in salted water to cover. Bring to a boil over medium heat. Reduce heat and simmer for 3½ hours. Skim surface of liquid from time to time.

Add plantains and sweet potatoes. Cook slowly for about 20 minutes, or until vegetables are tender. Remove pigs' ears and vegetables from liquid. Reserve ½ cup of liquid. Cut pigs' ears into strips.

In a heavy skillet, combine pigs' ears, vegetables, ½ cup of reserved liquid, and all other ingredients. Simmer for 20 minutes. Serve hot, with pigeon peas and green salad. *Serves 4.*

Vegetables

Breadfruit Puffs

1 half-ripe medium breadfruit   2 egg yolks
1/2 cup flour   1/2 cup milk
1 tablespoon baking powder   1 tablespoon grated onion
pinch of salt   corn oil for deep frying

Peel and core breadfruit and cut into 8 slices. Cook in salted boiling water to cover for 20 minutes. Drain and cool.

Sift together flour, baking powder, and salt. In a separate bowl, beat egg yolks and add milk and grated onion. Pour egg mixture into dry ingredients, stirring gently until well blended.

Heat oil in a heavy skillet. Dip breadfruit slices in batter and deep fry in hot oil for about 3 minutes on each side. Place on paper towel to remove excess oil. Serve warm, as part of a main course, as you would potatoes. *Serves 8.*

Stuffed Christophene

Christophene, also known as chayote, choyote, or chuchu, is a pear-shaped vegetable, 3 to 4 inches long with light green skin covered with deep wrinkles and fine prickles. The flesh is pale green or whitish and has a firm, smooth texture. Christophene belongs to the squash family and can be cooked as you would zucchini or any other delicate squash.

4 christophenes
1/8 pound lean ground beef
1/2 medium onion, chopped
1 stalk celery, chopped
1/4 medium green pepper, chopped
2 drops Tabasco (or to taste)
salt to taste

1/8 teaspoon freshly ground pepper
1/2 teaspoon crushed thyme
1/2 cup cooked ham, minced
2 tablespoons butter
2 tablespoons olive oil
1 egg yolk
1/2 cup breadcrumbs

Preheat oven to 350°.

Scrub christophenes gently to remove surface prickles. *Do not peel outer layer of skin.* Slice christophenes in half lengthwise. Place in boiling salted water to cover. Cook for about 5 minutes. Remove from water and scoop out pulp, being careful not to break the shells. Place shells in a shallow baking dish.

In a skillet, cook ground beef until light brown. Remove from skillet and set aside. Sauté onion, celery, and green pepper in beef grease until tender. Pour off grease.

In a bowl, mash the pulp of the christophenes and mix with beef, sautéed vegetables, Tabasco, salt, pepper, thyme, and ham. Combine butter and oil in a heavy pot. Add christophene mixture. Beat egg yolk and add to mixture until well blended. Cover and simmer for 5 minutes.

Fill christophene shells with mixture and sprinkle with breadcrumbs. Bake until golden brown, about 3 to 5 minutes. *Serves 8.*

Vegetable and Ham Casserole

1/4 *pound christophene, peeled*
  and cubed
1/2 *pound sweet potato, peeled*
  and cubed
1/2 *pound tannia seed, peeled and*
  cubed

1 1/2 *cups fresh green peas, cooked*
1 *cup cooked ham, chopped*
1 *cup milk*
1 *tablespoon butter*
2 *tablespoons cheddar cheese,*
  grated

Preheat oven to 350°.

Place christophene, sweet potato, and tannia seed in salted boiling water to cover. Boil for 15 minutes, or until tender. Grease a medium-sized casserole. Put vegetables and ham in casserole, alternating a layer of vegetables and a layer of ham. Add milk. Dot top with butter and bake for 10 minutes. Add cheese and bake for another 3 to 5 minutes, until cheese is golden brown. *Serves about 6.*

Pigeon Peas and Rice

1 1/2 cups dried pigeon peas
1/4 pound salt pork, diced
2 medium onions, chopped
1 stalk celery, chopped
1/2 cup green pepper, seeded and
   chopped
1 hot red pepper, seeded and
   chopped

1 clove garlic, chopped
6 cups water
1/4 teaspoon thyme
1/4 teaspoon freshly ground black
   pepper
1/4 teaspoon fresh parsley, chopped
2 cups rice

Soak pigeon peas overnight in 3 to 4 cups of cold water. Drain and rinse peas.

In a heavy pot, sauté salt pork until golden. With a slotted spoon remove salt pork and set aside. In the same skillet, sauté onions, celery, green and red pepper, and garlic until onion is tender. Add salt pork, peas, water, thyme, pepper, and parsley. Bring to a boil, then reduce heat. Simmer until peas are tender. Add rice and stir. Cover and simmer for about 30 minutes, or until all liquid is absorbed. Serve with meat or fish. *Serves 8.*

Stewed Pigeon Peas

1 pound dried pigeon peas
1 clove garlic, crushed
3 tablespoons olive oil
2 tablespoons butter
1/4 pound uncooked ham, chopped
1 medium onion, sliced

1 stalk celery, chopped
1 tomato, chopped
1 teaspoon white sugar
dash of black pepper
1/4 teaspoon thyme
salt to taste

Soak peas overnight in 3 to 4 cups of cold water. Drain and rinse peas.

In a heavy pot, combine peas, garlic, and 1 cup of boiling water. Cover and simmer until peas are tender, about 20 minutes. Add a little hot water if necessary to prevent burning.

In a skillet, heat olive oil and butter over a moderate flame and sauté ham, onion, and celery until onion is tender. Add contents of skillet to peas along with tomato, sugar, pepper, thyme, and salt and a little warm water if needed to cover. Simmer for 10 minutes. *Serves 6.*

Stuffed Green Peppers

4 medium green peppers
1/8 pound lean ground beef
1 tablespoon butter
2 tablespoons olive oil
1 medium onion, chopped
1 stalk celery, chopped
1/2 cup breadcrumbs

salt to taste
1/8 teaspoon pepper
1/2 cup cooked ham, minced
2 drops Tabasco
1/2 teaspoon crushed thyme
1 egg, beaten
4 teaspoons grated cheese

Preheat oven to 350°.

Cut off tops of peppers; remove seeds and membrane and discard. Place peppers in boiling water to cover and cook for about 3 minutes. Drain. Place peppers in a well-greased baking dish.

In a skillet, sauté ground beef until lightly browned. With a slotted spoon remove beef and set aside. Pour off grease and wipe skillet. In the same skillet, heat butter and olive oil over a moderate flame. Add chopped onion and celery and sauté until tender. Remove vegetables with a slotted spoon and pour off grease.

In a bowl, mix beef, vegetables, breadcrumbs, salt, pepper, ham, Tabasco, thyme, and beaten egg. Stir and blend well. Fill peppers with mixture and sprinkle tops with grated cheese. Bake until cheese is melted, about 5 minutes. *Serves 4.*

Stuffed Eggplant

4 firm medium tomatoes, not
  quite ripe
1/2 teaspoon Tabasco
2 tablespoons lemon juice
1/8 teaspoon pepper
salt to taste
1/2 teaspoon crushed thyme
1/4 cup parsley, chopped
2 tablespoons olive oil

1 tablespoon butter
1 medium onion, chopped
1 stalk celery, chopped
1/4 medium green pepper, chopped
1/4 pound fresh baby shrimp,
  shelled and deveined
1 egg, beaten
1/2 cup breadcrumbs

Preheat oven to 350°.

Slice eggplants in half lengthwise. Place in salted boiling water to cover. Boil for about 5 minutes, or until tender. Remove from water and scoop out pulp, being careful not to break the skins. Place skins in a well-greased baking dish.

In a bowl, mash the eggplant pulp and mix in Tabasco, breadcrumbs, thyme, salt, and pepper. In a heavy skillet, sauté ground beef until lightly browned. Remove meat with a slotted spoon and set aside. Pour off grease and wipe skillet. In the same skillet, heat butter and olive oil over a moderate flame. Add chopped vegetables and sauté until vegetables are tender. Remove vegetables with a slotted spoon.

Add vegetables, ground beef, and cooked ham to eggplant mixture. Add eggs and blend with mixture. Fill eggplant skins with mixture and sprinkle with cheese. Bake until cheese is melted, about 5 minutes. *Serves 8.*

Stuffed Tomatoes

4 firm medium tomatoes, not
  quite ripe
1/2 teaspoon Tabasco
2 tablespoons lemon juice
1/8 teaspoon pepper
salt to taste
1/2 teaspoon crushed thyme
1/4 cup parsley, chopped
2 tablespoons olive oil

1 tablespoon butter
1 medium onion, chopped
1 stalk celery, chopped
1/4 medium green pepper, chopped
1/4 pound fresh baby shrimp,
  shelled and deveined
1 egg, beaten
1/2 cup breadcrumbs

Preheat oven to 350°.

Cut off tops of tomatoes and discard. Remove and set aside pulp, being careful not to break the skins. Place tomatoes in a well-greased baking dish.

In a bowl, mash the tomato pulp and mix in Tabasco, lemon juice, pepper, salt, thyme, and parsley. In a skillet, heat olive oil and butter over a moderate flame. Add chopped onion, celery, and green pepper and sauté until vegetables are tender. Remove vegetables with a slotted spoon and set aside. In the same skillet, sauté shrimp until they turn pink, about 1 to 2 minutes.

Add sautéed vegetables and shrimp to tomato mixture. Add egg and blend with mixture. Fill tomatoes with tomato mixture and sprinkle with breadcrumbs. Bake until breadcrumbs are golden brown, about 3 to 5 minutes. *Serves 4.*

Omelets
and
Pancakes

Banana Pancakes

1/4 cup flour
1/2 teaspoon baking powder
1 tablespoon cinnamon
2 egg yolks, beaten
1/4 cup milk
1 tablespoon vanilla extract

4 ripe bananas, mashed
2 tablespoons butter, melted
2 egg whites, stiffly beaten
butter or margarine for griddle
confectioners' sugar (optional)

Sift together flour, baking powder, and cinnamon. In a separate bowl, combine egg yolks, milk, and vanilla extract. Pour into dry ingredients and stir well. Stir in bananas and butter. Fold in egg whites and blend gently. Let batter settle for a few minutes.

Drop batter, 2 tablespoons at a time, on a hot, buttered griddle and cook until golden brown on each side. Or, if you prefer, divide batter into 4 portions and make 4 large pancakes. For an added touch, sprinkle with confectioners' sugar. *Serves 4.*

Pumpkin Pancakes

1 cup flour
1/2 teaspoon baking powder
4 tablespoons sugar (or to taste)
1 teaspoon salt
1 teaspoon cinnamon
2 eggs, lightly beaten

2 cups milk
1 teaspoon vanilla extract
2 pounds pumpkin, mashed or
    pureed
corn oil for frying

Sift together flour, baking powder, sugar, salt, and cinnamon. In a separate bowl, combine eggs, milk, and vanilla. Pour into dry ingredients. Stir in pumpkin and blend well. Heat corn oil in a heavy skillet or griddle. Drop batter, 2 tablespoons at a time, into skillet. Cook until golden brown on each side. Drain on paper towel. *Serves 4.*

NOTE: Winter squash, such as Hubbard, acorn, or butternut squash, may be substituted for pumpkin.

Ma Chance's Shrimp Pancakes

1/4 cup flour
1/2 teaspoon baking powder
1 egg, beaten
1/4 cup milk
1 tablespoon butter, melted
1 tablespoon fresh parsley,
  chopped

salt and pepper to taste
1 medium onion, chopped
corn oil for frying
3 drops Tabasco
7 ounces baby shrimp, drained
  and finely minced

Sift together flour and baking powder. In a separate bowl, combine egg, milk, butter, parsley, salt, and pepper. Pour into dry ingredients and blend well.

In a skillet, sauté onion in corn oil until tender. Add Tabasco and shrimp and cook for 2 to 3 minutes, or until raw look is gone. Remove shrimp mixture with a slotted spoon and set aside.

Pour batter into a clean, lightly greased skillet. Cook for about a minute, until batter thickens. Flip pancake. Add shrimp filling in center of the pancake. Fold pancake from edge to edge and cook until golden brown on each side. Cut into portions and serve. *Serves 4 to 6.*

Lobster Omelet

2 tablespoons butter
2 tablespoons olive oil
1 medium green onion, chopped
1/2 pound lobster meat, minced
6 eggs, lightly beaten
1/2 cup milk
black pepper to taste
salt to taste
Tabasco to taste

1 1/2 teaspoons parsley, chopped
1 large tomato, sliced
1 green pepper, sliced in rounds
1 tablespoon butter for frying

GARNISH
2 tomatoes, sliced
1 green pepper, sliced

In a heavy skillet, heat 2 tablespoons of butter and olive oil over a moderate flame and sauté onion and lobster until onion is golden. Remove onion and lobster with a slotted spoon and drain on paper towel.

Gently beat eggs and milk together until light and airy. Add pepper, salt, Tabasco, and parsley. Pour mixture into a lightly greased omelet pan. Fry over low heat until omelet begins to set. Add lobster and onion. Rotate pan slightly in circular motion. Tilt pan to a 45° angle and gradually fold or roll omelet onto itself, enclosing lobster filling, and cook until firm. Serve with tomato and green pepper. Serves 6.

Shrimp Omelet

4 eggs
1/2 cup milk
1 small onion, grated
1/2 teaspoon crushed thyme
1/2 red pepper, chopped
1/4 teaspoon ground pepper

1 7-ounce can baby shrimp,
  drained, or 3/4 cup fresh baby
  shrimp
1 tablespoon butter for frying
1 tablespoon olive oil (for fresh
  shrimp)

Gently beat eggs and milk until light and airy. Blend with all other ingredients *except* shrimp. Pour into a lightly greased omelet pan.

Fry over low heat until omelet begins to set. Add baby shrimp. Rotate pan slightly in circular motion. Tilt to a 45° angle and fold or roll omelet onto itself, enclosing shrimp, and cook until firm. *Serves 2 to 3.*

NOTE: If using fresh shrimp, sauté in hot olive oil for 1 to 2 minutes.

Ma Chance's Oyster Omelet

6 slices bacon
2 dozen fresh oysters, drained
1/4 cup flour
1/4 teaspoon baking powder
6 large eggs
1/4 teaspoon parsley, chopped

salt to taste
pepper to taste
1/4 teaspoon lemon juice
1/4 teaspoon chives, chopped
Tabasco to taste
1 tablespoon butter for frying

In a heavy skillet, fry bacon until crisp and set aside. Pour off grease from skillet, leaving enough to sauté oysters.

In the same skillet, sauté oysters until golden brown on both sides, about 2 to 3 minutes. Remove with a slotted spoon and place on paper towel to remove excess oil.

In a bowl, sift together flour and baking powder. In another bowl, beat eggs until blended. Add to dry ingredients. Add seasonings, lemon juice, chives, Tabasco, and oysters. Blend well.

Pour mixture into a lightly greased omelet pan. Fry over low heat until omelet begins to set. Crumble bacon and add to omelet. Fold omelet and cook until firm. *Serves 3 to 4.*

Cassava Bread

2 cups cassava, finely grated
1 teaspoon salt
1/4 cup dark brown sugar

3/4 cup coconut, finely grated
dash of vanilla extract
1 tablespoon corn oil

In a bowl, mix cassava and salt. Place mixture in a damp cloth and squeeze out all of the liquid. Add sugar, coconut, and vanilla extract to cassava and mix thoroughly. Mold cassava mixture into a ball and flatten with hands.

Heat oil in a skillet. Place flattened cassava dough in skillet and cook until golden brown, about 2 minutes on each side. Drain on paper towel. Serve with fish or soup or a glass of milk, with stewed fruit or syrup. *Serves 6.*

Johnnycake #1

Johnnycakes can be eaten either hot or cold, with butter, jam, syrup, or honey. I prefer them hot with butter.

Legend has it that johnnycake was originally called "journeycake." It was prepared by women before their husbands set off for work in the morning. It could be made quickly and provided quick energy as a meal in the middle of the day.

Now johnnycake is served at breakfast or brunch, or as a complement to an entrée. Johnnycakes are excellent served with soups or as a snack with a glass of milk.

One of the best qualities of johnnycake is that it stays fresh for several days after it is prepared. Try it.

2 cups all-purpose flour
2 teaspoons baking powder
1/4 teaspoon salt
1 teaspoon sugar

1 tablespoon shortening or butter
1/4 to 1/2 cup water
1/2 cup corn oil for frying

In a mixing bowl, sift together flour, baking powder, salt, and sugar. Add water, a little at a time. Mixture will begin to get sticky. Knead dough with hands until loose flour is blended but dough is not clinging to fingers. If dough begins to cling, add a dusting of flour to bowl and roll dough in it. Continue kneading until smooth.

Dust a cutting board with flour and gently roll dough into a long roll about 1 1/2 to 2 inches in diameter. Cut into 1-inch pieces. Roll each piece into a ball about the size of a lime. Flatten balls gently with your palms or with a floured rolling pin.

Heat about 1/8 inch of oil in a skillet. Slowly fry johnnycakes to golden yellow on both sides. Remove from skillet and drain on paper towel. Serve hot. *Makes about 1 dozen.*

NOTE: For a delicious variation, use cream-style corn instead of water. Or you may use milk, buttermilk, half and half, or coconut milk instead of water.

Johnnycake #2

1/2 cup warm water
1/2 tablespoon active dry yeast
2 cups all-purpose flour
1/4 teaspoon salt

1 teaspoon sugar
1 tablespoon shortening
1 1/2 tablespoons butter

Preheat oven to 350°.

Pour warm water into a small bowl and sprinkle in yeast. After a few minutes, stir to dissolve the yeast. Set aside in a warm place.

In a mixing bowl, sift together flour, salt, and sugar. Cut in shortening and butter and blend until mixture is grainy. Add yeast liquid to dry ingredients and mix to make a soft dough. Add more lukewarm water or flour if needed for desired consistency.

Knead on a lightly floured board for 4 to 6 minutes, or until dough is smooth. Return to bowl, cover, and let stand in a warm corner of the kitchen for about 1 hour, until dough has risen.

Gently mold dough into balls about 1 1/2 inches in diameter. Place on a cookie sheet, cover with a damp cloth, and let stand for 1 hour in a warm place.

With a floured rolling pin, flatten balls until they are approximately 1/4 inch thick. Prick each with a fork in any pattern that pleases you. Bake in the oven for 15 to 20 minutes, or until they are golden brown. Serve hot. *Makes about 1 dozen.*

Desserts

People in Grand Case, as in many other places in the world, have a sweet tooth. An evening meal is not complete without dessert.

Carrot and Fruit Cake

1 cup dried mixed fruit (pears,
   peaches, apricots), diced finely
1/2 cup shelled walnuts, chopped
1 cup raisins
1/2 cup rum
2 cups flour
1 teaspoon baking soda
1 teaspoon baking powder

1/2 teaspoon ground ginger
1 teaspoon ground cinnamon
1/2 teaspoon ground cloves
3 eggs
1/2 cup sugar
1 cup corn oil
1 1/2 cups carrots, coarsely grated

Preheat oven to 325°.

Soak dried mixed fruit, walnuts, and raisins in rum to cover for 30 minutes.

In a large bowl, sift together flour, baking soda, and baking powder. Mix in ginger, cinnamon, and cloves and set aside. In a separate bowl, beat eggs lightly, then gradually add sugar and oil. Fold in carrots and sifted ingredients, beating just enough to blend. Add rum mixture to cake batter. Stir and mix well.

Pour batter into a greased and lightly floured 9" x 12" x 2" pan and bake for 1 hour. Cool thoroughly.

Raisin Pound Cake

1/2 cup raisins
1/8 cup rum
1 cup sugar
1/2 cup butter

6 eggs, separated
1 cup flour
1 tablespoon baking powder
1 teaspoon vanilla extract

Preheat oven to 325°.

Soak raisins in rum for 30 minutes.

In a large mixing bowl, blend sugar and butter until butter is creamy. Add egg yolks to butter mixture. Beat egg whites until stiff, then add 1/2 of egg whites to butter mixture and mix thoroughly. Fold in balance of egg whites. Sift together flour and baking powder and stir slowly into mixture. Add vanilla extract and raisins. Stir and mix well.

Pour batter into two 9" x 9" greased and lightly floured pans. Bake until cakes shrink from edges, about 20 to 30 minutes. Cool before removing from pans.

Black Cake
(FRUITCAKE)

2 pounds seedless raisins, finely chopped

1 1/2 pounds prunes, finely chopped

1 1/2 pounds currants, finely chopped

1/2 pound glazed lemon peel, grated

1/2 pound glazed papaya skin, or 1/2 pound glazed lime peel, grated

1/2 pound citron, grated

1/2 pound glazed orange peel, grated

1 pound candied red cherries

1/2 pound walnuts, finely chopped

1/2 pound almonds, finely chopped

3/4 cup cognac

1 cup dark rum

1 bottle (4/5 quart) cherry liqueur

4 cups all-purpose flour

2 teaspoons cinnamon

1 teaspoon ground cloves

3/4 teaspoon mace

2 teaspoons nutmeg

1/2 teaspoon baking soda

1 pound butter, unsalted

1 pound dark brown sugar

15 large eggs, separated

1 cup unsifted flour to dust fruits and nuts

In a large earthenware or glass bowl, combine raisins, prunes, currants, lemon peel, papaya skin or lime peel, citron, orange peel, cherries, walnuts, and almonds. Pour cognac, rum, and cherry liqueur over fruits and nuts. Blend well. Cover and set aside for at least 3 to 4 days, preferably for a week.

Preheat oven to 275°.

In a large mixing bowl, sift together all-purpose flour, cinnamon, cloves, mace, nutmeg, and baking soda. Set aside. In another bowl, cream butter until soft. Gradually add sugar and cream until very light. Beat egg yolks and add to butter mixture, mixing thoroughly. Beat egg whites until stiff. Fold into the butter mixture. Stir until well blended. Fold in the flour mixture and blend well.

Pour off liquid from fruit and nut mixture. Dust fruits and nuts with unsifted flour and toss to mix. Shake off excess flour in colander or strainer then fold into cake mixture. Stir until well blended.

Line two 10-inch loaf pans or six 5 1/2-cup ring mold pans with buttered brown paper. Pour batter into pans, filling each about halfway.

Bake for 1 hour and 45 minutes to 2 hours. Test with a toothpick to determine when cakes are done. The toothpick should be free of batter when withdrawn from the centers of the cakes.

When thoroughly cooled, remove cakes from pans. Wrap in cheesecloth, then in aluminum foil. Place in airtight containers. Unwrap and sprinkle cakes with cognac every 10 to 12 days for at least 6 weeks. *Yields about 12 pounds.*

Sweet Potato Pudding

3 pounds sweet potatoes, peeled
    and grated coarsely
3/4 to 1 cup sugar
1/4 pound pumpkin (winter
    squash), peeled, seeded, and
    grated coarsely
1/2 cup butter, melted
1 teaspoon ground cinnamon
4 egg yolks, beaten

2 to 2 1/2 cups milk
1/4 cup flour
2 tablespoons vanilla extract
1/2 teaspoon ground nutmeg
1/4 teaspoon allspice
1/4 teaspoon ground black pepper
1/2 cup seedless raisins
2 tablespoons rum or brandy
4 egg whites, stiffly beaten

Preheat oven to 350°.

Mix together all ingredients *except* egg whites and blend well. Fold in egg whites. Bake pudding in a greased baking dish for about 1 hour. It may be served warm or cold, topped with whipped cream or ice cream. *Makes about 12 servings.*

Rice Pudding

1/2 cup raisins

1/8 cup rum

2 cups cooked rice

1 1/2 cups milk

1 tablespoon soft butter

4 tablespoons sugar (or to taste)

3 eggs, beaten

1 teaspoon vanilla extract

1/2 teaspoon salt

1/4 teaspoon nutmeg

1 teaspoon cinnamon

Preheat oven to 325°.

Soak raisins in rum to cover for 30 minutes.

Combine rice, milk, butter, sugar, eggs, vanilla, and salt and blend well. Add nutmeg and raisins mixture. Combine these ingredients lightly with a fork. Pour mixture into a greased baking dish. Sprinkle top with cinnamon. Bake until set, about 50 minutes. *Serves 6 to 8.*

Gooseberries-on-Stick

Gooseberries are round, firm, tart berries that are greenish-yellow in color and grow to about 1 inch in diameter.

4 cups gooseberries

2 cups water

2 cups sugar

2 sticks cinnamon

Remove stems and blossom ends from gooseberries and prick berries with a fork. Place in water to cover and let stand overnight in a covered bowl.

In a saucepan, combine water and sugar and bring to a slow boil over medium heat, stirring until sugar dissolves. Let a thick syrup form. Drain berries and add with cinnamon to syrup mixture. Simmer slowly for 15 to 20 minutes.

Remove berries from pot with a slotted spoon and let cool. String about 12 berries on a thin, 12-inch-long wooden skewer. *Makes enough for about 20 skewers.*

Stewed Papaya

1 half-ripe large papaya   1 cup sugar
1 cup water   1 teaspoon vanilla extract

Peel and quarter papaya and remove seeds. In a saucepan, combine
water and sugar and bring to a slow boil over medium heat, stirring
until sugar dissolves. Reduce heat and add vanilla extract and papaya.
Simmer for 5 minutes. Cool and serve. *Serves 4.*

Stewed Guavas

Guavas are the fruit of a tropical evergreen tree. They are about 4
inches in diameter with yellow or dark pink flesh. You can eat them
fresh or make them into preserves and relishes, and they add an
interesting flavor to chutney.

1 cup water   *¹/₂ stick cinnamon, broken into*
1 cup sugar   *small pieces*
6 ripe guavas, cut in half and
   seeds removed

In a saucepan, combine water and sugar and bring to a slow boil over
medium heat, stirring until sugar dissolves. Reduce heat, add guavas
and cinnamon, and simmer for about 30 minutes. Remove guavas.
Cool and serve guavas with a little of the syrup. *Makes about 6 servings.*

Stewed Cashew Fruit

The tropical fruit known as cashew is used for this recipe. The kernel of the cashew fruit yields cashew nuts. In Brazil the cashew fruit is called caju.

12 *ripe cashews*   2 *cups sugar*
9 *cups water*   2 *sticks cinnamon*

Remove and discard the seeds of the cashews. Prick the skin of each fruit several times with a fork and squeeze out the juice, which is extremely tart and bitter. Place fruit in a saucepan.

Bring 5 cups of the water to a boil in a separate pot and pour over the fruit. When cashews have cooled enough so that you can handle them comfortably, squeeze out the water.

In a saucepan, combine the remaining 4 cups of water, sugar, and cinnamon and bring to a boil for 5 minutes, stirring until sugar dissolves.

Place cashews in syrup mixture, stirring gently from time to time to prevent sticking. The fruit should remain intact. Reduce heat and simmer for 30 minutes. Remove from heat. Cool and place in a covered 1-quart jar. Refrigerate until thoroughly chilled. *Makes about 6 servings.*

Stewed Mangoes

The mango is a luscious fruit of an evergreen tree grown in tropical and semi-tropical countries. When ripe, its color varies from green to a deep rose red, and the flesh is an orange yellow. Mangoes are very popular in the Caribbean. They are eaten fresh and are made into relishes, ice cream, drinks, and preserves.

4 half-ripe medium mangoes   *1 cup sugar*
1 cup water   *1 teaspoon vanilla extract*

Peel mangoes, remove seeds, and quarter. In a saucepan, combine water and sugar and bring to a slow boil over medium heat, stirring until sugar dissolves. Let a thick syrup form. Reduce heat, add mangoes and vanilla extract to syrup mixture, and simmer for about 10 minutes. Cool and serve. *Serves 8.*

Stewed Tamarinds

Tamarinds are cinnamon-brown in color and 2 to 6 inches long. Their acid pulp is eaten fresh and is used in chutney and curry.

12 half-ripe tamarinds   *2 sticks cinnamon*
1 cup water   *1/2 teaspoon vanilla extract*
1 cup sugar

Cut tamarinds in half, peel, and remove seeds. Cover with water and let stand overnight. The next day, drain. If any acid taste remains, place tamarinds in water to cover and boil for 5 minutes. Drain well. Dry on paper towel.

In a saucepan, combine water, sugar, and cinnamon and bring to a boil over medium heat, stirring until sugar dissolves. When a medium thick syrup has formed, add tamarinds and vanilla extract. Remove from heat when syrup reaches 200° on a candy thermometer. The syrup should be jellylike and the tamarinds should be soft. If the syrup is too thick, add a little water. Cool. Place in covered jars. Refrigerate until thoroughly chilled. *Serves 4.*

Almond Candy

The almond tree is a beautiful, shady tree that bears almonds by the thousands when in season. There are many almond trees on St. Martin. In fact, I have one in my front yard, and my first restaurant was built around an almond tree.

Peanuts may be substituted for almonds in this recipe, if you prefer.

4 cups white or brown sugar
1 stick cinnamon
1 cup water

1 pound whole almonds or
peanuts

In a saucepan, combine sugar, cinnamon, and water and bring to a boil over medium heat, stirring constantly until sugar dissolves. Add almonds to syrup mixture, lower heat, and cook until a candy thermometer reaches 250°, stirring regularly. Remove from heat.

On a cutting board or piece of marble thoroughly dampened with water, drop 1 or 2 tablespoons of mixture at a time, depending on size desired. Let stand about 1 hour, until hardened. *Makes about 2 dozen.*

Coconut Candy

1 fresh medium coconut, grated   ¼ teaspoon almond extract
1½ cups water   red food coloring (optional)
3 cups sugar

Preheat oven to 325°.

Poke out 3 eyes of the coconut and drain liquid inside. Place coconut in oven until shell cracks, about 20 minutes. Remove from oven and take off shell. Peel coconut meat and grate.

Stir water and sugar in a heavy saucepan and cook over medium heat until sugar dissolves. Add grated coconut and simmer until mixture becomes hard around the edges, at about 230° on a candy thermometer. Remove from heat and add almond extract (substitute cinnamon, if desired). Remove 2 or 3 tablespoons of the mixture, add food coloring to desired shade, and set aside for decoration.

Sprinkle a large wooden cutting board or piece of marble lightly with water. Drop about 2 tablespoons of the mixture at a time on the board, depending on the size you like. Make round or oval shapes. Place a little of the colored mixture in the center of each piece. Let candy harden until it can be removed easily. *Makes about 1 dozen.*

Coconut Pie

1/4 cup seedless raisins
rum to cover raisins
1 cup sugar
1/2 cup water
1/2 teaspoon vanilla extract
1/2 teaspoon almond extract
1 teaspoon cinnamon, or
  2 1/2 sticks cinnamon, broken
  into small pieces

2 cups coconut, grated
1/2 cup butter, melted
2 eggs, lightly beaten
1 pie crust (see recipe below)
1/4 cup heavy cream

Preheat oven to 350°.

Soak raisins in rum to cover for 30 minutes.

In a double boiler, combine sugar, water, vanilla extract, almond extract, and cinnamon. Cook over moderate heat, stirring constantly. Stir in coconut, butter, and eggs. Simmer for 15 minutes or less, covered. Remove mixture from heat. Add raisin and rum mixture and blend well. Cool.

Pour mixture into unbaked pie crust. Place strips of crust over pie. Trim edges. Brush crust with heavy cream. Bake in oven for 30 to 40 minutes, until crust is golden. Serve with whipped cream or ice cream. *Makes one 10-inch pie.*

SWEET PIE CRUST

1 1/2 cups flour
1/4 teaspoon baking powder
pinch of sugar
8 tablespoons butter
1/2 cup solid shortening or
  margarine

1 large egg
3 to 5 tablespoons cold milk
1/2 teaspoon vanilla extract
1 teaspoon cinnamon

In a large mixing bowl, sift flour, baking powder, and sugar. Add butter and shortening and work into the flour until mixture resembles coarse meal. In a separate bowl, mix egg with milk, vanilla extract, and cinnamon. Gradually add to flour mixture.

Flour hands lightly. Mix ingredients until dough forms a ball. If dough seems too dry, add another tablespoon of milk. On a lightly floured cooking board, roll the dough to 1/8-inch or 1/4-inch thickness. Place dough in a pie pan. Trim excess. Use trimming to make decorative strips with which to cover the top of the pie. *Makes one 10-inch pie crust.*

Pineapple Pie

1 fresh, ripe medium pineapple   1/2 teaspoon almond extract
1 cup water   1 egg yolk, lightly beaten
1/2 cup sugar   1 pie crust (see recipe on p. 135)
1/2 teaspoon vanilla extract   1/4 cup heavy cream

Preheat oven to 350°.

Peel and crush pineapple. In a double boiler, combine water, sugar, vanilla extract, and almond extract. Cook over moderate heat, stirring constantly. Stir in pineapple and egg. Simmer for 15 minutes or less, uncovered. Remove mixture from heat. Cool.

Pour mixture into unbaked pie crust. Place strips of crust over pie. Trim edges. Brush crust with heavy cream. Bake in oven for 30 to 40 minutes, until crust is golden. *Makes one 10-inch pie.*

Coconut Drops

1/4 cup butter
1 cup sugar
1 fresh medium coconut, grated
2 eggs
1 teaspoon vanilla extract

1 cup milk
1 cup flour
1/2 teaspoon baking powder
1/2 teaspoon cinnamon
dash of salt

Preheat oven to 350°.

In a mixing bowl, blend butter and sugar until creamy. Beat in coconut, eggs, vanilla extract, and milk. In a separate bowl, sift together dry ingredients; add to coconut mixture and blend well.

Drop about 2 tablespoons of the mixture at a time on a lightly greased cookie sheet. Bake until golden brown, about 15 to 20 minutes. *Makes 2 dozen.*

Tropical Fruit Supreme

1 cup mango, diced
1 cup papaya, diced
1 cup fresh pineapple, diced

1 cup bananas, sliced
1/4 cup dark rum
1/4 cup coconut, grated

In a bowl, combine all ingredients *except* coconut and blend thoroughly. Chill for at least 2 hours. Serve in dessert dishes or goblets. Garnish with grated coconut. *Serves 6 to 8.*

Mango Magique

2 cups mango pulp, mashed
1 cup sugar
1 1/2 teaspoons unflavored gelatin

1/2 cup water
2 tablespoons lime juice, chilled
2 cups heavy cream

In a mixing bowl, combine mango pulp and sugar. Soak gelatin in 1/4 cup of cold water. Add 1/4 cup of boiling water and blend until gelatin is dissolved. Let both mixtures stand for 15 minutes.

Add mango mixture and chilled lime juice to gelatin and blend thoroughly. In a separate bowl, whip heavy cream and fold into mixture. Pour into a mold, cover, and place in freezer for at least 1 hour, no longer than 24 hours. Remove from freezer 30 minutes before serving. *Serves 8.*

Beverages

These punches are so delicious and soothing to the throat that many people are tempted to drink them down fast. But they are very potent and should be sipped slowly. They are generally served chilled, in small portions before dinner. They can also be served over ice. Either dark or white rum can be used, and you should experiment with the amounts of sugar and rum until you find a combination whose taste pleases you.

Guavaberry Punch

The guavaberry, a small, flavorful fruit, is found in only a few islands in the West Indies. It grows on a hardwood tree, with a silver-gray trunk, that may be 30 feet tall.

The berry is one-half to one-inch in diameter and may be dark red or yellow. The darker berry gives a stronger flavor; the yellow is relatively mild.

The tree produces berries once a year, from October to December, and the punch is traditionally a Christmas drink in St. Martin.

Guavaberry punch should not be confused with sorrel, a punch made from the sepals of a tropical flower and often served at Christmas on many Caribbean islands.

2 cups guavaberries
3 quarts rum

2 cups sugar syrup (see recipe below)

Wash guavaberries. Place berries and rum in a 1-gallon glass jar and set aside for a week or more. The longer the better. Some people soak them from one year to the next.

Pour rum from the berries. Discard berries. Add sugar syrup. Refrigerate until chilled and serve over crushed ice. Add a fresh cinnamon stick to each glass when serving. *Serves 15 to 20.*

SUGAR SYRUP

2 cups water
2 cups sugar
2 sticks cinnamon

In a saucepan, slowly bring water, cinnamon sticks, and sugar to a boil. Stir to prevent scorching. Occasionally brush the sides of the pot with a pastry brush dipped in cold water to prevent formation of sugar crystals. Boil slowly until a soft-ball stage is reached, 10 to 15 minutes. Remove cinnamon sticks and discard. Syrup can be stored in a covered jar in the refrigerator. *Yields 2 cups.*

Prickly Pear Punch

The prickly pear is also known as the cactus pear, Indian fig, and Barbary fig.

6 prickly pears   *3 cups rum*
1 cup sugar   *1 teaspoon vanilla extract*
1 cup water   *red food coloring*

Prickly pears have sharp spines that should be removed by singeing. Then pare, quarter, and core pears. Remove seeds and reserve.

Add fruit, seeds, and sugar to water and simmer until a thick syrup forms. Remove from heat and strain through a double thickness of cheesecloth to make certain no seeds find their way into the punch.

Add rum, vanilla extract, and enough food coloring for desired effect. Chill until ready to serve. *Yields about 1 quart.*

Strub
(MA CHANCE'S LIME PUNCH)

This punch is a favorite among my guests.

¹/₂ cup fresh lime juice   *¹/₂ cup water*
¹/₄ to ¹/₂ cup sugar   *4 cups rum*

In a saucepan, mix lime juice, sugar, and water. Stir over medium heat until sugar is dissolved and mixture reaches a soft-ball stage. Remove from heat and add rum. Chill. Serve over ice with a slice of lime. *Yields 5 cups.*

Creole Fruit Punch

This is a very satisfying beverage to serve at parties.

2 medium mangoes, cubed
1 cup cherries
6 plums, cut in half
1 cup guavaberries
1/2 pound seedless prunes, cut in
   half

2 limes or lemons, sliced
sugar to taste
4 cups Dubonnet
1 cup white rum
1 1/2 quarts water

Put all ingredients in a 2-gallon jar and let stand for 1 day at room temperature. Chill and serve over ice. *Yields about 3 1/2 quarts.*

Soursop Juice

Also known as prickly custard apple or guanabana, the soursop is a large, heart-shaped fruit, delicately flavored, with a soft, cottony flesh. Soursops can be enjoyed plain, sprinkled with sugar, or made into sherbets or ice cream. The juice of the soursop added to milk or water (and sugar if desired) makes a refreshing drink. Serve chilled with a grating of nutmeg.

Papaya Juice

The papaya is a fragrant tropical fruit with a taste between that of a Cranshaw melon and that of a peach. It is large and oblong in shape and when fully ripe, the flesh is a golden yellow-orange color and the greenish rind has turned soft and yellow. It is best to buy papayas when half ripe and let them ripen on the kitchen counter. Once ripe, a papaya should be kept in the refrigerator, where it will stay fresh for a week.

The papaya can be eaten raw, boiled as a vegetable, or preserved. Its juice is delicious as well as nutritious. On St. Martin we call papayas "pawpaws." They are also called frutas, bombas, and lechosas.

1 ripe papaya
milk to taste
sugar to taste

Peel papaya, cut in half, remove seeds. Cube and put in blender with milk and sugar to taste. Blend until smooth. Serve chilled and garnished with slices of lime. *Yields approximately 8 ounces.*

Passion Fruit Punch

5 *passion fruits, unpeeled*   4 *cups water*
1/2 *cup sugar*   1/4 *cup dark rum*

Remove seeds from passion fruits and cut into small pieces. Place in a bowl. In a separate bowl, combine and blend sugar, water, and rum. Pour over fruit and blend thoroughly. Let mixture stand covered for 3 to 4 hours.

Crush and strain fruit, preserving liquid only. Chill. Serve with a twist of lime and ice. *Makes 6 glasses.*

NOTE: Extra rum or brandy may be added to taste.

Menus

Brunch or Luncheon Menus

LOBSTER OMELET
TOSSED GREEN SALAD
STEWED PAPAYA

FISH SOUP
BREADFRUIT SALAD
MANGO MAGIQUE

STUFFED CHRISTOPHENE
COLE SLAW
TROPICAL FRUIT SUPREME

MA CHANCE'S SHRIMP PANCAKES
TOSSED GREEN SALAD
STEWED GUAVAS

CRAB FRITTERS
STUFFED TOMATOES
GOOSEBERRIES-ON-STICK

CONCH AND PAPAYA
BREADFRUIT SALAD
CARROT AND FRUIT CAKE

LOBSTER SALAD WITH LIME JUICE
JOHNNYCAKES
RICE PUDDING

CODFISH AND VEGETABLE SALAD
STEWED MANGOES

AVOCADO DIP
CHICKEN SALAD
STEWED TAMARINDS

BANANA FRITTERS
LOBSTER SALAD # 2
PINEAPPLE PIE

SHRIMP OMELET
TOSSED GREEN SALAD
SWEET POTATO PUDDING

CODFISH FRITTERS
FRESH FRUIT SALAD
RAISIN POUND CAKE

MARINATED GRILLED CHICKEN
STEWED PIGEON PEAS
TOSSED GREEN SALAD
STEWED TAMARINDS

CHICKEN CHOW SOUP
CRABMEAT-STUFFED EGGS
CARROT AND FRUIT CAKE

TANNIA SEED FRITTERS
RED SNAPPER FILLETS
SLICED AVOCADO
MANGO MAGIQUE

STUFFED CLAMS
TUNA AND MACARONI SALAD
TROPICAL FRUIT SUPREME

OYSTER CORNMEAL FRITTERS
COLE SLAW
SWEET POTATO PUDDING

Dinner Menus

MA CHANCE'S CREOLE SOUP
POT-ROASTED LEG OF GOAT
TOSSED GREEN SALAD
RICE PUDDING

FISH SOUP
MARINATED GRILLED CHICKEN
COLE SLAW
PINEAPPLE PIE

CHICKEN CHOW SOUP
LOBSTER WITH HOT CORN BALLS
CARROT AND FRUIT CAKE

SALT CODFISH BALLS
PICKLED PIGS' EARS AND
VEGETABLES
STUFFED TOMATOES
GOOSEBERRIES-ON-STICK

BEEF PATTIES
CODFISH AND EGGPLANT
BREADFRUIT PUFFS
ASSORTMENT OF ALMOND AND
COCONUT CANDIES
STEWED MANGOES AND GUAVAS

BANANA FRITTERS
STUFFED BAKED FISH
COLE SLAW
SWEET POTATO PUDDING

PEANUT SOUP
CONCH AND CURRY RICE
COCONUT PIE

CRAB FRITTERS
BEEF AND DUMPLINGS
TOSSED GREEN SALAD
RAISIN POUND CAKE

WHELK SALAD
ROAST LEG OF GOAT
STUFFED TOMATOES
PINEAPPLE PIE

MA CHANCE'S FISH CHOWDER
MARINATED GRILLED CHICKEN
STUFFED CHRISTOPHENE
STEWED PAPAYA

STUFFED ESCARGOTS
RED SNAPPER FILLETS
PIGEON PEAS AND RICE
TOSSED GREEN SALAD
SWEET POTATO PUDDING

DEVILED CRAB DELUXE
TURTLE STEW
TOSSED GREEN SALAD
CARROT AND FRUIT CAKE

MA CHANCE'S OYSTER OMELET
CALF'S FOOT SOUP
STEWED TAMARINDS

CODFISH AND VEGETABLE SALAD
POT-ROASTED LEG OF GOAT
JOHNNYCAKES
STEWED PAPAYA

CALALOO SOUP WITH DUMPLINGS
FRIED CODFISH
TOSSED GREEN SALAD
CARROT AND FRUIT CAKE

OYSTERS IN VINEGAR SAUCE
STUFFED EGGPLANT
POACHED KINGFISH
RAISIN POUND CAKE

MUTTON SOUP
CONCH AND PAPAYA
STUFFED TOMATOES
TOSSED GREEN SALAD
PINEAPPLE PIE

CRABMEAT ROYALE
MA CHANCE'S CHICKEN AND
SHRIMP CREOLE
TOSSED GREEN SALAD
COCONUT PIE

CRABMEAT-STUFFED EGGS
CHICKEN AND DUMPLINGS
STUFFED CHRISTOPHENE
STEWED MANGOES

FISH SOUP
MARINATED GRILLED CHICKEN
STUFFED TOMATOES
GOOSEBERRIES-ON-STICK

TURTLE SOUP
STEWED CODFISH WITH EGGS
AND TOMATOES
TOSSED GREEN SALAD
TROPICAL FRUIT SUPREME

Buffet Dinner:
BEEF PATTIES
SALT CODFISH BALLS
STEAMED CHERRYSTONE CLAMS
CRAB FRITTERS
FRIED CLAMS
CHICKEN SALAD
LOBSTER SALAD #2
SELECTION OF RUM PUNCHES
SELECTION OF PIES AND CAKES
ASSORTMENT OF STEWED AND
FRESH FRUITS

Sources for Ingredients

Some of the ingredients called for in my recipes will not be found in typical North American food stores, especially in smaller communities. They often may be found, however, in Spanish or other ethnic markets. In addition, Goya and La Preferida are brand names to look for that offer canned or packaged foods from the Caribbean.

Sometimes, hard-to-find ingredients can be ordered by your local food store or grown at home. Or they may be obtained by mail from importers who specialize in unusual ingredients.

The following are some purveyors who may be able to provide some of the more unusual ingredients needed for these recipes:

California
Casa Lucas Market
2934 24th Street
San Francisco, CA 94110

Mi Rancho Market, Inc.
3365 20th Street
San Francisco, CA 94110

District of Columbia
Pena's Spanish Store
1636 17th Street N.W.
Washington, DC 20009

Florida
The Delicatessen, Burdine's
    Dadeland Shopping Center
Miami, FL 33156

Epicure Market, Inc.
1656 Alton Road
Miami Beach, FL 33139

Imperial Super Market
5175 S.W. Eighth Street
Miami, FL 33134

Illinois

La Preferida, Inc.
3400 West 35th Street
Chicago, IL 60632

Marshall Field & Company
111 N. State Street
Chicago, IL 60602

Iowa

Swiss Colony
Lindale Plaza
Cedar Rapids, IA 52402

Louisiana

Central Grocery Company
923 Decatur Street
New Orleans, LA 70116

Progress Grocery Company
915 Decatur Street
New Orleans, LA 70116

New York

Casa Moneo Spanish Imports
210 West 14th Street
New York, NY 10011

Kalustyan Orient Export
Trading Corporation
123 Lexington Avenue
New York, NY 10016

H. Roth and Son
1577 First Avenue
New York, NY 10028

Ohio

Spanish & American Food
Market
7001 Wade Park Avenue
Cleveland, OH 44103

Texas

Antone's Import Company
Box 3352
Houston, TX 77001

Jim Jamail & Sons Food
Market
3114 Kirby Drive
Houston, TX 77098

Pier 1 Imports
5403 South Rice Avenue
Houston, TX 77081

Index

Codfish
  and curry rice, 78
  and dumplings, 79
  and eggplant, 78
  fried, 79
  fritters, 25
  salad, 64
    with vegetables, 61
  stew, with eggs and tomatoes, 77
Cole slaw, 66
Conch
  and curry rice, 83
  and macaroni, 82
  and papaya, 81
  soup, 50
  stew, 81
Cornmeal
  balls, lobster stew with, 75
  and oyster fritters, 30
Court bouillon, 88
Crabmeat
  burgers, 76
  deluxe, 84
  dip, 39
  eggs stuffed with, 38
  fritters, 31
  royale, 85
Creole soup, 43
Curry rice
  codfish and, 78
  conch and, 83

Deviled crab, 84
Dinner menus, 150–51
Dips
  avocado, 38
  crab, 39
Dumplings
  beef and, 99
  calaloo soup with, 45–46

chicken and, 94
codfish and, 79

Eggplant
  codfish and, 78
  stuffed, 111
Eggs
  codfish stew with, 77
  crabmeat-stuffed, 38
Escargots, stuffed, 36

Fish
  chowder, 48
  fillets, 74
  poached, 73
  soup, 47
  stuffed baked, 71
  and vegetable casserole, 72
  See also Codfish
Fritters
  banana, 29
  breadfruit, 27
  codfish, 25
  crab, 31
  oyster cornmeal, 30
  pumpkin, 28
  tannia seed, 26
Fruit
  and carrot cake, 125
  punch, 143
  salad, 66
  tropical, supreme, 137
Fruitcake, 127–28

Goat
  head and foot soup, 55
  leg of
    pot-roasted, 101
    roast, 100

Sugar syrup, 141
Sweet potato pudding, 128

Tamarinds, stewed, 132
Tannia seed fritters, 26
Tomatoes
  codfish stew with eggs and,
    77
  stuffed, 112
Tossed green salad, 68
Tuna and macaroni salad, 65
Turtle
  soup, 49

steak, 86
stew, 87

Vegetables
  codfish salad with, 61
  and fish casserole, 72
  and ham casserole, 107
  pickled pigs' ears and, 102
Vinegar sauce, oysters in,
    34

Whelk salad, 62